Intermediate

Quick Work

Teacher's Book

Vicki Hollett

OXFORD
UNIVERSITY PRESS

Great Clarendon Street, Oxford OX2 6DP

Oxford University Press is a department of the University of Oxford. It furthers the University's objective of excellence in research, scholarship, and education by publishing worldwide in

Oxford   New York

Auckland   Bangkok   Buenos Aires   Cape Town   Chennai
Dar es Salaam   Delhi   Hong Kong   Istanbul   Karachi
Kolkata   Kuala Lumpur   Madrid   Melbourne   Mexico City
Mumbai   Nairobi   São Paulo   Shanghai   Singapore   Taipei
Tokyo   Toronto

with an associated company in Berlin

Oxford and Oxford English are registered trade marks of Oxford University Press in the UK and in certain other countries

© Oxford University Press 2001

The moral rights of the author have been asserted

Database right Oxford University Press (maker)

First published 2001
Second impression 2002

All rights reserved. No part of this publication may be reproduced, stored in a retrieval system, or transmitted, in any form or by any means, without the prior permission in writing of Oxford University Press (with the sole exception of photocopying carried out under the conditions stated in the paragraph headed 'Photocopying'), or as expressly permitted by law, or under terms agreed with the appropriate reprographics rights organization. Enquiries concerning reproduction outside the scope of the above should be sent to the ELT Rights Department, Oxford University Press, at the address above

You must not circulate this book in any other binding or cover and you must impose this same condition on any acquirer

Photocopying

The Publisher grants permission for the photocopying of those pages marked 'photocopiable' according to the following conditions. Individual purchasers may make copies for their own use or for use by classes that they teach. School purchasers may make copies for use by staff and students, but this permission does not extend to additional schools or branches

Under no circumstances may any part of this book be photocopied for resale

Any web sites referred to in this publication are in the public domain and their addresses are provided by Oxford University Press for information only. Oxford University Press disclaims any responsibility for the content.

ISBN 0 19 457297 8

Printed in Spain

Acknowledgements

The authors and publisher are grateful to those who have given permission to reproduce the following extracts and adaptations of copyright material:

pp 46–7 'GE brings good managers to life' by Cathy Olofson. Appeared in *Fast Company* Issue 18, page 72. Reproduced by permission of Fast Company.
p 49 'How IBM gets unstuck' by Liz Zack. Appeared in *Fast Company* issue 28. Reproduced by permission of Fast Company.
p 49 'Encourage wild ideas' by Tia O'Brien. Appeared in *Fast Company* issue 2. Reproduced by permission of Fast Company.
p 50 'Business Behaviour' from www.williamsinference.com. Reproduced by permission of Williams Inference Centre.
p 63 Extract from *When Cultures Collide* 2nd Edition by Richard Lewis (ed.), Published by Nicholas Brealey Publishing, London, 1999. www.nbrealey-books.com' Reproduced by permission of Nicholas Brealey Publishing.

Contents

Introduction   4

1 Exchanging information   7

2 Sharing ideas   16

3 Tackling problems   21

4 Planning ahead   30

5 Resolving conflict   37

Photocopiable activities 43

Introduction

The course

Quick Work Intermediate is a short Business English course with a flexible design which allows you to use it in large classes, and small group and one-to-one teaching contexts. The course can be completed in approximately thirty classroom hours and can be used in the following ways:

- as a short intensive course to be completed in approximately one week of full-time study
- as a resource for extensive courses taking place over a period of weeks or months
- from beginning to end – the language work ranges from basic to more complex as the book progresses
- as a dip-in resource – each section of the book is free-standing, so sections can be selected and used out of sequence according to the needs of particular students.

As the name suggests, *Quick Work* is a short pacy course and the main emphasis throughout is on developing speaking and listening skills. It takes a time-efficient, task-based approach where each unit concentrates on developing business communication skills and language skills in key performance areas such as exchanging information, tackling problems, and planning. The activities reflect the kinds of task that learners typically need to perform in English in international work environments, and opportunities are provided for the learners to relate the tasks to their own personal work situation. Grammar and language work are provided on a 'need to know' basis to facilitate clear communication in particular contexts. These materials will allow you to draw on your students' professional knowledge, experience, and expertise to animate discussions and other communication activities.

The units

The five units of *Quick Work* follow a broadly similar format. Each one is divided into five or six different sections, which all reflect the general theme of the unit. Each section is slightly different to ensure different skills are tackled effectively and that there is variety within the units. A typical section within a unit might include:

- an **input task**, a reading and/or listening text, e.g. listening to a telephone call or reading a document
- **vocabulary lists** explaining key vocabulary from the input material
- a **language focus**, drawing attention to a feature of the English language and providing practice
- a **quick check** section, which is a short quiz-type activity to test students' knowledge of various language points and identify areas that may require further study
- a **task** where students are given the opportunity to practise new language and develop communication skills in a work-related activity.

The final section of each unit is a work-related task that requires the students to draw on and employ language and skills covered in earlier sections of the unit. In this way it provides an opportunity for revision and consolidation.

Other features

There are a number of additional features at the back of the Student's Book. You may wish to draw your learners' attention to them at the start of the course.

Information files (pages 56–62) These contain additional information for pair work activities and suggested answers to some exercises. Directions for when to use the information in the files appears at the appropriate point in the units of the Student's Book.

Tapescript (pages 63–68) This includes scripts of all the listening material.

Language notes (pages 69–74) These notes provide brief but clear information on the key language points covered in the book. Directions to the relevant pages of this section are given at appropriate points in the units.

Glossary (pages 75–79) In addition to the vocabulary notes which accompany the listening and reading activities, this glossary provides a useful additional resource for students during and after the course. It covers over 300 common business-related terms contained in the Student's Book.

As well as the Student's Book and this Teacher's Book, *Quick Work* also consists of a Workbook with additional language practice activities and a grammar reference file, and a choice of audio cassette or audio CD. The Workbook is an excellent addition for further practice during the course, or for revision and self study when the course is completed. Teachers and students with Internet access will also find free additional downloadable and online materials at www.oup.com/elt/quickwork.

International English

Many students of business English need to work in international contexts where they will be talking to other non-native speakers of English, rather than native speakers all the time. To prepare students for this, the recordings contain a good variety of non-native accents, as well as native accents. *Quick Work* focuses on language that is acceptable in both British and American English, so that learners are equipped with variety that will stand them in good stead in as much of the world as possible.

Further recommended materials

Although *Quick Work* provides the essential materials learners need to complete this short course, they may find the following resources useful:

- an up-to-date learner's dictionary, such as the *Oxford Advanced Learner's Dictionary* (also available on CD-rom)

- a business English dictionary, such as the *Oxford Dictionary of Business English for Learners of English*, for learners interested in financial vocabulary and stockbroking terminology
- an authoritative grammar reference book, such as Michael Swan's *Practical English Usage* (OUP)
- a business English grammar practice book, such as Michael Duckworth's *Grammar and Practice* (OUP).

Teacher's Book and photocopiable materials

This teacher's book provides a range of suggestions for exploiting the course material effectively. It acts as a guide through various exercises, and offers optional ideas for extending the activities and adapting them to different classroom situations. It provides extra guidance for teachers who are new to teaching Business English, and some ideas that we hope will be stimulating for experienced business English trainers too.

There are photocopiable materials at the back of this book which can be used to supplement the activities in the Student's Book. You will find notes on how to use them in the unit teaching notes in this book, together with answers where necessary.

Working with *Quick Work*

Business and professional English learners

Business and professional English learners bring a range of skills and expertise to the learning situation, which *Quick Work* exploits. It is a highly interactive course and the majority of the activities involve pair or group interaction. It is designed to draw on the learner's experience and ideas, and maximize their opportunities for and exposure to spoken English. A key feature of the course is its task-based syllabus, which ensures students are engaged in realistic and practical work tasks, allowing them to make major contributions to the lesson content.

Input activities

There is generally a lead-in task preceding the input texts, which will help to prepare students for listening or reading. If you think your students may have difficulty with a listening or reading task, you might want to preview some of the key vocabulary or phrases listed beside the text.

The listening and reading activities usually involve a global comprehension task, followed by a task seeking more specific information. You may need to allow students to listen to a recording or read a text several times. Encourage your students to take notes, particularly in listening tasks. If a listening text proves particularly difficult, you can refer students to the tapescript. There are tapescripts for all the listening texts at the back of the Student's Book.

Language work

All courses should be tailored as specifically as possible to the individual needs of the learners and *Quick Work* will give you a head start in this. The language syllabus encompasses key vocabulary, and grammar and usage points for intermediate students, and its task-focused syllabus encourages them to apply the language they learn to their own work situations. By setting tasks that mirror those the learners will need to perform in their jobs, the practical relevance of the language work is ensured.

The Student's Book takes an inductive approach to grammar and vocabulary. It develops learners' understanding of English language systems by highlighting important features and asking questions that encourage deeper thought and exploration. Answers to the questions raised can be found in the language notes at the back of the Student's Book, along with further points of interest to learners at this language level.

Task preparation and repetition

Evidence from second language acquisition research suggests that students will not only perform more accurately, but they will also employ a wider range of linguistic structures if we give them time to prepare before speaking tasks. Instructions for student preparation are generally provided in the Student's Book.

There is also evidence that repeating tasks is very important for acquisition. Depending on how students perform a task, you may wish to ask them to repeat it after you've given feedback. The second time around your students will have already mastered the mechanics of the task, so they can concentrate more on how they are communicating and the improvement can be very rewarding.

Pair work and group activities

How you organize group activities and tasks will depend on many different factors including the time available, the personalities and interests of your students, the mood of the moment, etc. But plainly, the number of students in your class is a crucial factor. If you are teaching one-to-one classes, you will need to participate in many of the activities yourself. With a class of six or fewer you can run many activities, particularly meetings, as a whole class activity. With large classes, you will want to divide students into groups. So, for example, you might have the same meeting running simultaneously in different groups.

When setting up speaking tasks, you may want to hand over as much control as possible to the students. For example, you will probably want to appoint a student to chair a meeting rather than do it yourself. This will involve the students more and provide them with more opportunities for managing discussions and communication practice. It will also allow you more time to monitor their output, so you can provide helpful feedback.

Introduction

Students who talk too much and too little

When you're running the tasks in *Quick Work*, you will want to ensure that everybody participates as fully as possible. Here are some ideas that may help when dealing with students who talk too much or too little:

- Establish equal participation as a goal at the start of a task and evaluate the groups' success in achieving it at the end.
- Alternatively, set consensus as a goal and tell the group they are jointly responsible for ensuring everyone's views are heard, discussed, and taken account of.
- Set a short task and keep a record of who spoke for how long. Then show your results to the students for discussion.
- Give the members of a group tokens that represent a certain amount of talking time, e.g. 30 seconds' talking costs one token.
- Slip private notes to students in the middle of discussions with instructions that will encourage others to talk, e.g.:
  Ask Jan to tell everyone about …
  Find out what Marcus and James feel about …
  Similarly, quiet students can be slipped notes saying things such as:
  Suggest …
  Ask everyone if they'd like you to summarize what's been agreed so far?
- Before a lesson starts or after it's finished, have a private chat with a dominant speaker and ask them to help you in encouraging more reticent class members to talk. Similarly, have a word with a quiet student and discuss ways in which they might be helped to participate more.

English in the classroom

In monolingual classes, students may be tempted to use their first language as they become engaged in performing the tasks. You may need to remind them that the goal in the task-based activities is to improve their communication skills in English and seek agreement that English should be adopted as the classroom language.

Feedback and correction

Feedback and correction is a major part of our job as business English teachers, and also one of the most difficult. There are no hard and fast rules about how it is best accomplished but here are some points to bear in mind:

Linguistic accuracy is only one aspect of effective communication and it may be equally or more important to evaluate issues such as structuring of ideas, body language, or cultural awareness. One way of doing this is to picture yourself in a business role when you're assessing your students' performance in a task. For example, if your student is role-playing a conversation with a potential customer, you might try to imagine yourself as the customer and consider what their impression might be.

The task-based syllabus of *Quick Work* will provide you with excellent opportunities for evaluating your students' performance in terms of successful business outcomes. So, for example, in a telephone role-play task such as the one in Complaints, Unit 3, rather than focusing on linguistic accuracy, you can evaluate performance in terms of how effectively the complaint was made and dealt with. So your criteria might be:

Completion Were all the items of contention on the invoice mentioned, fully understood, and resolved? (i.e. Did they get the job done?)

Timing Was the task performed without unnecessary delays? (Time costs money!)

Manner Was the existing business relationship damaged, maintained, or improved by the exchange? (Upsetting customers or suppliers is generally bad for business.)

You may find linguistic issues come up as you evaluate with criteria like this. For example, mistakes with vocabulary or grammar could cause miscommunication, which might affect the **timing**, if not the **completion** of the task. Pronunciation, and particularly intonation, is likely to be an important factor in **manner**. But evaluating a student's performance in terms of business outcomes enables you to focus on the essentials rather than details that might be unimportant or insignificant for your students.

When students are performing speaking tasks, you will need to record points you want to draw attention to later simply by taking notes, or using a tape recorder, or video. Keeping a record ensures things don't get forgotten and it gives you the valuable option of providing feedback after the event rather than during it.

At the end of activities, try to involve your students in the feedback. You might begin with general questions like:

What did you think of that task?
Do you think that went well?
Was it useful? Why?
Was it easy/difficult? Why?
What would you do differently next time?

You can ask students to discuss their feelings about a task in pairs if you think saying things in front of the group might inhibit them.

After seeking general reactions, you might want to ask what happened during the task. *How did the conversation start? What happened next?*, etc. This will give you a chance to refresh everyone's memories about the different elements of the conversation and raise questions about any things that were said or motivations that were unclear to you. As well as commenting on problem areas, try to ensure you provide positive feedback on good performance as well. Remember you can comment on success in terms of achieving business outcomes and draw attention to good behaviour and expressions you heard.

1 Exchanging information

Language work

The six sections of this unit look at:
- Present tenses: simple, continuous, and perfect
- Collocations with *make* and *do* (and *take* as an extension activity)
- Checking understanding
- Countable and uncountable nouns
- Public speaking techniques and structuring talks
- Restating and rephrasing questions
- *raise* and *rise*, *say* and *tell*

GETTING ACQUAINTED

Business and professional learners are generally keen to make a good first impression on new business contacts. They will welcome the opportunities given in this section to practise introducing themselves and other people. This section also allows you to find out more about students' needs and priorities.

1 More detailed getting to know you activities are coming later in this section, so don't spend longer on this exercise than necessary. Your goal here is to ensure students know one another's names and companies, and have a rough idea of the fields their fellow class members work in.

Organize students into pairs or small groups to conduct the introductions as described in **1**. Group students who don't know one another well together. If all students know one another very well, you can skip this activity and move directly on to **2**.

Students who have never met before may be tempted to continue this activity for a long time. Reassure them that they will have the opportunity to get better acquainted throughout this lesson and set a time limit of three minutes or less.

2 This exercise gives students the opportunity to tell one another more about their work. *Quick Work* contains activities related to all these things and it will be helpful in your planning to make notes about which areas are likely to be of most interest to whom. In very small classes of three or four conduct this as a whole class activity. In larger classes, group students in pairs or small groups. If necessary, remind students to explain not only which things are related to their work, but also how they're related.

> **VARIATION**
> *If students know one another well, ask them to predict what they think the main focus of another student's job will be and why. They should then seek confirmation or correction from the other student.*

3 [1.1] Play the recording once and collect students' answers.

> **ANSWERS**
> The main focus of Tony's job is managing people.
> The main focus of Akiko's job is working with ideas.

Play the recording again and tell students to ask for help if there is anything they didn't catch. Ask students to stop you if they hear any useful phrases for making introductions, or alternatively direct them to the tapescript on page 63 and allow them to underline useful phrases for introductions while listening.

4 Elicit the answers to the questions.

> **ANSWERS**
> a 3   present perfect continuous
> b 2   present continuous
> c 1   present simple

Ask students to make up three similar sentences about themselves. Go round the class, collecting their sentences and correcting any errors. Direct attention to the present tense language notes on page 69. You may wish to take this opportunity to explain that there is information on all language questions in the language notes on pages 69–74.

5 Students can complete this exercise individually or in pairs.

> **ANSWERS**
> 1 comes from
> 2 has been working
> 3 's currently running
> 4 's spending
> 5 finds
> 6 has been teaching

6 These mini role-plays involve introducing yourself and introducing other people in a range of formal and

Exchanging information

informal settings. Exploit the pictures for class discussion, e.g.:

What relationships might the people have?
Is this a first meeting or not?
How formal will the language be?

Ask students to predict what the people in the pictures are saying and write any useful phrases you elicit on the board. Try to elicit both formal and informal introduction phrases, as well as phrases people might use to describe the people they are introducing, e.g.:

Formal	Informal
May I introduce you to …?	*Do you know …?*
Delighted to meet you.	*Nice to meet you.*
It gives me great pleasure to introduce …	*This is …*

General
Welcome to …
<name> works for …
<name> is responsible for …

If necessary, check students are familiar with British and American conventions for shaking hands the first time we meet someone. Contrast customs that might be different to customs in students' cultures.

Listen to students while they are role-playing the conversations and make notes so you can correct any mistakes in grammar, wording, or register and provide useful alternatives.

a This should be role-played in threes. In one-to-one classes, draw a third character on the board and play one character yourself.

b Students work in pairs, first interviewing their partner to establish a plausible talk topic and gather biographical information, then introducing the speaker. You could refer them to **5** for a model.

c and d These are both pairwork activities. Students can work with the same partner, or be instructed to move on to a new one. In large classes, you can call on pairs of students to act out their conversations in front of the class after they have rehearsed them.

Task

This is designed as a pairwork task, but it is simple to expand to three students if appropriate. It is a needs-analysis task that culminates in setting learning objectives for the course and it has very tangible benefits for you and your students in course planning. As has been mentioned before, the more you can learn about the things your students need to do in English and the difficulties they have, the better equipped you will be to tailor the activities in this book to the individuals in your class and allocate time effectively.

1 and **2** Make notes of the things you learn as students work through **1** and **2**. The skills listed in **2** correspond to the areas covered in the five different units of *Quick Work*.

3 Take notes from different pairs in a feedback session and assemble a list of objectives with the whole class on the board. If the list is hopelessly long, ask them to refine it and set priorities. Try to negotiate an agreement that everyone feels comfortable with. You may wish to adapt or change these objectives later, but they can be a useful starting point and reassure your students that their classes will help them meet their goals.

> *EXTRA ACTIVITY*
> *Turn to Activity 1 on page 43. This is a false facts game which builds group rapport and works equally well with students who know one another and students who don't.*

DESCRIBING CULTURE

This section allows students to learn more about one another's companies or departments. As it involves their perceptions and opinions of the values of their organizations, it is suitable for students working in the same or different organizations.

1 If necessary, explain that *What's the company you work for like?* means *Describe your company*. The adjectives in the box may prompt students to look for other adjectives, so be ready to provide them as required. For example, if the stocks and shares of your students' companies are not traded on a stock exchange, supply *privately-held* as an alternative to *publicly-traded*. Depending on the companies they work for, there may be other terms they need such as *family business*.

Help students to qualify their descriptions when appropriate, *e.g. We're a large company in our home market, but a medium-sized company in global terms.* Also ask them to explain the adjectives they have

Exchanging information

chosen when appropriate. For example, if they say their company is old-fashioned, ask in what ways.

If you need to, point out that we use the verbs *to nationalize* and *to privatize* to talk about what happens to companies, but we generally use the adjectives *nationalized* and *privatized* to describe an industry rather than a company, e.g. *the nationalized steel industry*.

> Note: The legal status of companies may also come up in discussion. Obviously these vary according to different legal systems around the world, but very broadly speaking Co.Ltd (Company Limited) in the UK is equivalent to Inc. (Incorporated) in the US, AG in Germany, etc. A parent company controls subsidiaries – other smaller companies. Subsidiaries may be wholly-owned or partly-owned by their parents. A holding company is a paper construct rather than a physical company, in that it doesn't actually produce or sell things. Its function is to control another company or companies through holding their shares.
>
> In American English, companies take singular verb forms. In British English singular or plural verb forms are equally acceptable. e.g.
> - *IBM makes computers.* (US English)
> - *IBM makes computers.* or *IBM make computers.* (British English)

2 You may wish to do this 'reverse dictionary' exercise to check that students know the meaning of the words in bold below. You should read these definitions aloud while students find the appropriate word in the list.

- working together, especially to create or produce something – **collaboration**
- the introduction of new things or ideas – **innovation**
- giving a lot of your time and attention to something because you believe it's right or important – **commitment**
- being truthful and having firm moral ideas – **integrity**

Encourage students to suggest other things their organizations value, e.g. quality.

3 Ask students to look at the pictures and to read the captions, then make brief notes of the values they predict on the board. Very often, students are able to predict very accurately: e.g. 3M – creativity and innovation; FedEx – customer service. Toyota is more difficult, but teamwork and collaboration, or quality are often suggested.

4 Return to **3** when students have read the texts, and review whether their predictions were correct. Students can find the answers to the questions individually or in pairs.

ANSWERS
a 1: Toyota; 2: FedEx; 3: 3M
b It would rather let its employees make mistakes than tell them how to do their jobs. To make 30% of revenues from products that didn't exist four years ago.
c To have a completely satisfied customer at the end of every transaction. The reward programme allows managers to make extra payments on the spot, and presumably it's to encourage employees to make extra efforts to take care of customers.
d Continuous improvement. Huge reductions in both costs and lead times.

5 Students' own answers.

6 These phrases will all be useful later on when students come to describe their corporate cultures. Draw attention to the way these phrases continue after the main verb.

We're committed **to** *(-ing)* …
We're constantly looking for ways **to** *(do)* …
It's our mission **to** *(do)* …
We're well known **for** … *(-ing)*

7 This is the first of several activities in the book which focus attention on common collocations.

ANSWERS
Toyota
No improvement is too small for us to make
to do things faster

Fedex
That's not easy to do
to make extra payments
doing something extra

3M
make mistakes
how to do their jobs

You will be looking at the differing meanings of *make* and *do* in the next exercise, but here are some other common expressions students may suggest:

Make
a suggestion, a request, arrangements, a complaint, a phone call, an offer, a profit, a loss, a decision, a purchase, preparations, an appointment, an effort, love, war, etc.

Exchanging information

Do
business, research, a job, someone a favour, a good turn

> Note: If students confuse *make* and *do*, this is a good opportunity to introduce the notion of collocation. Read the introduction to collocations in the language notes, page 73 with your class, and answer any questions they may have.
>
> Here are some points that may be helpful while working with students in this area:
>
> 1 Collocations are a matter of probability rather than possibility. For example, a verb such as *spend* collocates with *money* in that these two words co-occur more than is statistically likely. A verb such as *look at* could also co-occur with *money* but this is not as statistically likely. So *look at* and *money* are not collocates.
> 2 The strength of the magnetism varies between words. Collocations will vary as to how firmly fixed they are. Also, the linking between words within a collocation is not equally strong in both directions. *Mitigating* almost demands to be followed by *circumstances*, but *circumstances* could be preceded by a variety of other adjectives, such as *difficult*, *adverse*, *reduced*, *strange*, etc. All languages have collocations and students might be able to think of examples in their own language. Sometimes they can be directly translated into English. Sometimes they can't.
> 3 Collocation has received much attention in language learning in recent years. Many theorists suggest that students need to learn large numbers of common collocations to avoid their speech deviating from the norm.
> 4 There is some evidence that learning collocations and 'chunks' of language is of great value to the learner in that it aids retrieval from the memory. Processing may be easier if collocations are retrieved and then combined, improving fluency and consequently enhancing the learner's ability to focus on larger structures of discourse.
> 5 It's not always easy to tell whether words are collocations or not. If you and your students have seen certain words used together many times, the chances are they are collocations.
> 6 Good learners' dictionaries include common collocates in the example sentences they provide.

8 Students can work individually or in pairs to do this exercise.

> ANSWERS
> a earn
> b produce
> c force
> d perform an action
> e work
> f make progress or develop
> g perform an unspecified action

> *EXTRA ACTIVITY*
> *Another verb used in many expressions that students often confuse is* **take**. *For a similar exercise with* **take**, *see* **Activity 2** *on page 44.*

Task

1 If students are short of ideas, remind them that they might include:

a their organization's mission and what it believes in
b what it's well known for
c the things it's committed to and constantly trying to do.

Set a time limit of two or three minutes for preparation.

2 In small classes, this can be done as a whole class activity. Ensure students listen to one another's presentations carefully by asking them to think of questions to ask the presenters when they have finished.

> *EXTRA ACTIVITY*
> *For further practice in talking about organizational values and goals, turn to* **Activity 3** *on page 45 of this book. In small classes, it can be done in pairs. In large classes, it can be played as a game, with teams competing to get the most correct answers. Alternatively, you can give some students an objective and others an organization, and instruct them to mingle and find their partner.*
>
> *Answers: a a fire service, b a utility company, c a lottery organization, d a medical centre, e an environmental action group, f a public library, g an insurance company*

Exchanging information

QUESTIONING COSTS

This task prepares students to describe and ask and answer questions on common work place problems.

1 As in the Student's Book.

2 🔲 If you think students may have difficulty with the vocabulary in the listening text, go through the word list. If necessary, play the recording several times, pausing at appropriate points to collect answers.

> **ANSWERS**
> a Three
> b Ten
> c $2,000
> d Because Hamer has to bear several additional costs – a 15% surcharge for the right to select the better wood, and the costs of shipping the wood to Hamer's factory and then shipping rejected wood back to the mill.

Quick check

Do this before or after exercise 3. You may wish to refer students to the language notes on countable and uncountable nouns on page 73.

> **ANSWERS**
> 1 Uncountable:
>   equipment, information, data, news (If necessary, point out that that *s* does not indicate a plural form here.), research, traffic, pollution, work (If appropriate, point out that *work* is a noun as well as a verb.), advice, help
>   Countable:
>   fact, car, job, employee, person (The plural form is normally *people*. *Persons* is generally reserved for legal contexts.), suggestion
>   Countable or uncountable:
>   time (e.g. *How much time do we have?* (U) *How many times have you been to the US?* (C))
>   space (e.g. *There's plenty of space for your desk here.* (U) *There are only three parking spaces left.* (C))
>
> 2 a how much (U)   g not much (U)
>   b how many (C)   h a (C)
>   c a lot of (U/C)   i a couple of (C)
>   d plenty of (U/C)   j a little (U)
>   e lots of (U/C)   k a few (C)
>   f not many (C)   l some (U/C)

3 As in the Student's Book.

> **ANSWERS**
> 1 advice   8   time
> 2 information   9   wood
> 3 equipment   10 lot
> 4 wasn't   11 much
> 5 much   12 work
> 6 were   13 goes
> 7 few

4 🔲 This listening exercise draws attention to the fact that questions can be asked to check understanding as well as to get information. Point out that one of the most effective ways of checking we've understood a speaker is to repeat back what's been said and seek confirmation.

> **ANSWERS**
> Why are Hamer guitars so good? (information)
> Just three? (confirmation)
> How many people work here? (information)
> So, do you mean you wanted to get smaller? (confirmation)
> How much will that guitar cost? (information)
> So you reject more than two thirds of each shipment? (confirmation)

When playing the recording again, also draw attention to:

– the phrases the man uses to confirm she's right – *That's right, You got it.*
– the interaction noises that indicate the woman is interested: *Mmm, Uhuh*. Contrast them with similar sounds that might be made in your students' own language(s), if appropriate.

5 Be ready to explain to students that they will need to express the statements using different words. Also point out that rephrasing is a powerful way of checking we've understood what someone's said.

Give students plenty of practice time in pairs. Encourage students providing the prompts to confirm their partner's answers with phrases like: *Yes, That's right*, and *You've got it*.

Exchanging information

POSSIBLE ANSWERS
a So do you mean you don't use any machines?
b So do you mean you reject two thirds of the wood?
c So do you mean you're interested in the appearance and weight of the wood?
d So do you mean you have to bear the costs of shipping it both ways?
e So do you mean it takes a long time?
f So do you mean the wood selection requires experience?
g So do you mean you have no alternative?

6 This exercise can spark a great deal of discussion, so allow plenty of time. Students may ask you for vocabulary to describe different types of costs. If appropriate, explain:

Indirect costs or overheads are the regular costs of running a business, such as rent, salaries, electricity, telephone.
Direct costs are the costs of making a particular product or supplying a particular service, such as materials and labour.
Fixed costs are the overheads that don't change when more goods are made – e.g. rent, insurance, depreciation, office supplies.
Variable costs are the costs that increase with quantity when you're producing goods or providing a service.

Task

This is a pairwork information gap activity. Both students have access to the same budget figures but one has additional information about the costs. Before starting, give students enough time to read through their information and plan what they need to say.

When pairs have completed the activity, give feedback, then swap roles and repeat the activity.

PRESENTATION SKILLS

Making a presentation in your own language can be stressful, and making it in another language, doubly so. This section prepares students with some public speaking techniques and language for structuring talks.

1 Make notes on the board of any observations that students offer which can be used as criteria to evaluate the presentation they will hear in **2**. For example:

interesting topic
useful information
enthusiastic speaker
very clear

2 [1.3] Students working in the automotive industry, may be familiar with Dana. If so, collect any information they might know about the company from them before listening to the recording. Read through the questions then play all three sections of the recording right through without stopping. Encourage students to evaluate the speaker's performance, using the criteria you collected in **1**.

3 [1.3] Play the recording again, pausing at the end of each extract to collect answers.

ANSWERS
Extract 1
a Boston
b The Dana Corporation management style.
c Supplies automotive components.

Extract 2
d People are their most important asset.
e Forty hours of education a year.
f 43.3% of statistics are meaningless. (And quite possibly this statistic is one of the 43.3%!)

Extract 3
g Every person in the organization is encouraged to submit at least two ideas for improvements per month.
h 80%
i Students' own answers.

4 and **5** These exercises draw attention to common lexical phrases and collocations frequently used in public speaking. Students can do both exercises individually or in pairs. If students find **4** difficult, tell them to move on to **5** and then go back.

ANSWERS
a 3 start the talk
b 4 refer to visuals
c 1 go on to another topic
d 2 link similar points
e 6 refer back to a previous point
f 5 announce the topic of the talk

Exchanging information

6 🔲 Make sure students have read all the techniques before playing the recording. Pause where appropriate to collect answers.

> **POSSIBLE ANSWERS**
> **Extract one**
> b interacts with the audience:
> *Can I ask you all a question? How many of you have heard of the Dana Corporation? Can you raise your hand if you have? Excellent. Thank you.*
> c lists points in threes:
> *We'll look at who we are, what we do, and how we do it.*
> e asks a rhetorical question:
> *So, who is Dana? Dana is one of the largest automotive component suppliers in the world.*
>
> **Extract two**
> c lists points in threes:
> *We believe in education, participation, and innovation.*
> f uses a quotation or joke:
> *Now, you know what people say about statistics, don't you? 43.3% of statistics are meaningless.*
>
> **Extract three**
> a stresses or repeats key words and phrases:
> *And that's why we always say: communicate, communicate, communicate.*
> d pauses for effect:
> *Think about it. Two ideas a month times 86,000 employees worldwide …*

7 Public speakers frequently employ formulaic language and this exercise provides an opportunity for students to learn some standard phrases and check the appropriacy of things they might want to say.

> **POSSIBLE ANSWERS**
> a At the start:
> *Good afternoon, ladies and gentlemen.*
> *I'm delighted to be back in Manchester.*
> *Welcome to our Philadelphia plant.*
> *It gives me great pleasure to be with you today.*
>
> At the end:
> *You've been a wonderful audience.*
> *It's been a pleasure talking to you.*
> *Thank you very much.*
>
> b
> *You'll have an opportunity to ask questions at the end.*
> *Please save any questions you might have until the end.*
> *Feel free to interrupt if you have any questions.*
> *Please stop me if you'd like to ask a question.*
> *I'll be happy to take questions as we go along.*

8 The cartoons will prompt students with ideas. Encourage students to suggest other mistakes that may not appear in the cartoons.

> **POSSIBLE ANSWERS**
> − Obstructing the audience's view of visual aids
> − Unclear visual aids
> − Poor timing
> − Distracting body language
> − Lack of enthusiasm or animation

Task

The final section of this unit is a more extensive presentation task, so keep the presentations in this section brief. Set a time limit of just two or three minutes per presentation. If students encounter situations where they have to make impromptu talks, you could also put them under similar time pressure with preparation.

HANDLING QUESTIONS

For many business and professional learners, making presentations is the easy bit. Handling questions at the end is daunting. This section addresses this problem. You may wish to do the *Quick check* at the beginning of this section or later on when it is suggested.

1 Students' own answers.

2 🔲 Play the recording once through without stopping, then play it again, pausing where appropriate to collect answers.

> **ANSWERS**
> a The ship date deadline.
> b The original ship date was June 4th and it's now July 2nd.
> c A development problem – the product is coming out simultaneously in 31 countries and 9 languages so it's complicated.
> d Yes – the last two.
> e As projects become more complex, they require more work.
> f They are finishing a study of the development process and are looking for short cuts and ways to make improvements.

Exchanging information

13

> **POSSIBLE ANSWERS**
> This problem will be familiar to many students involved in project work. The speaker implies it is a scheduling problem, but some students may not see this as a good enough explanation for the delay. Presumably, if there's more work to be done on new releases, more time or resources should be allocated to the tasks and quite possibly the real problem is poor time estimates.

3 🔊 1.4 The questions in the recording occur in the same order as the similar questions appear in the list. Play the recording again pausing when appropriate to collect answers. Make sure students understand all these questions. They will need to use similar questions later when they perform the final task.

> **ANSWERS**
> a What's the ship date for this release?
> b Sorry, what was that?
> c What's causing this problem?
> d Are you asking about this release, or the previous releases?
> e Are these development problems getting worse?
> f Who is responsible for these delays?
> g Could you tell us what steps you're taking to deal with this?

Draw attention to the way two of these questions were used to clarify what people said. (b and d)

4 Point out that sometimes it's necessary for speakers to clarify questions before they can answer them, either because they didn't actually hear the question or because they didn't fully understand it. Explain that these phrases can be helpful in doing this, then do the exercise with the class.

> **ANSWERS**
> a didn't hear
> b didn't understand
> c didn't understand
> d didn't hear
> e didn't hear
> f didn't understand
> g didn't understand

5 This exercise is a drill-type activity that practises common lexical phrases employed when discussing problems. It also demonstrates a technique for deflecting unwanted questions, or simply signalling an important issue.

> **POSSIBLE ANSWERS**
> I think the important question is …
> a … how can we solve the problem.
> b … what are we going to do about it.
> c … how are we going to avoid long term damage.
> d … what can we do to stop it from happening again.
> e … what can we learn from this mistake.

Quick check

This can be done before or after **6**, or at the start or end of the section.

> **ANSWERS**
> 1 *raise* is regular and *rise* is irregular
> 2 a raise
>   b rise
>   c raise
>   d raise
> 3 a rise
>   b raise

---

6 Again, this exercise provides common lexical phrases often used by public speakers when dealing with questions. Some thoughts can match several speech bubbles, so tell students they must match each thought to only one phrase to find the best solution.

> **ANSWERS**
> a 3   e 7
> b 6   f 5
> c 1   g 2
> d 4

Point out that these expressions buy time for the speaker to think about their response to a question. Ask students to underline any sentences they would find useful. See if they can suggest any similar ways of saying these things, e.g. *That's tough to answer in a few words. Perhaps we could come back to that at the end if we have time.*

Task

1 When students have selected a problem, explain they will need to announce what the problem is to the class, but after that, their task is only to answer the questions the other students ask. They should not be making a presentation of the problem.

Exchanging information

2 As well as using the question prompts in the book, students can ask any other question they feel is relevant.

In small classes, this task can be repeated several times with students taking questions on a different problem each time.

EXTRA ACTIVITY
For more practice in forming questions and presentations, see Activity 4 on pages 46–7.

MAKING A PRESENTATION

This is the culminating task of the unit and it recycles much of the work that has gone before. It's a personalized task, in the sense that students can pick a presentation topic that relates directly to their own work. Success in this task is a great confidence booster, so try to ensure the activity ends on a triumphant note.

1 If necessary, explain that *tips* are pieces of advice. Invite students to ask any questions they might have about the tips before evaluating them. Encourage them to give examples of things they've learnt from their own experience of giving presentations.

2 Presentations vary greatly in their goals, audiences, levels of formality, size, and scope. The information you collect here will be useful in guiding students to make a presentation that they might need to make in their work place.

3 As in the Student's Book. This exercise reminds students that messages are tailored to a particular audience.

ANSWERS
a 2   d 4
b 5   e 3
c 1

4 This exercise encourages discussion of ways in which technical and managerial presentations might differ. The answers are highly debatable.

POSSIBLE ANSWERS
a senior managers
b engineers
c senior managers and engineers
d engineers
e senior managers
f engineers
g senior managers

Quick check

ANSWERS
a tell   g tell
b say   h tell
c say   i say
d tell   j tell
e say   k tell
f say

5 Ensure students realize that they should be keeping their audience secret. When they deliver their presentations to their colleagues, their colleagues will be asked to guess who the audience is.

6 This is a challenging exercise and some students may be tempted to write a paragraph. Insist on only ten words or less so that students are compelled to employ the KISS principle. (See the list in **1**.)

7 Involve students in the decision of how long they should have to prepare. You might wish to give them until the next lesson if they wish to prepare overhead or PowerPoint® slides.

8 In small classes, this can be conducted as a whole class activity. At the end of each presentation, encourage applause, congratulate the speaker, and find out:
– who students thought the audience was
– what the message was
– and invite them to ask the presenter questions.

Then give feedback yourself.

EXTRA ACTIVITY
You may wish to give students copies of Activity 5 on page 48 which is a presentation evaluation form for students to use when they are listening to other students' presentations. This activity should only be used in a supportive atmosphere, where it can improve concentration when listening and build confidence and rapport. Encourage students to give 'positive criticisms'.

Exchanging information

2 Sharing ideas

Language work

The five sections of this unit look at:
- Strong and weak suggestion forms
- Prepositions in phrases with gerunds
- Active and passive voices
- Expressions for explaining consequences
- 1st and 2nd conditional forms
- Phrases for discussions
- Multiword verbs

GENERATING IDEAS

This section involves students in brainstorming activities where they will need to make and respond to suggestions with differing degrees of force.

1 Use the questions to make sure everyone is familiar with brainstorming procedures. Ask how they might encourage creativity.

ANSWERS
Generally speaking, in brainstorming sessions people do not:
b Judge ideas one by one as people think of them.
d Follow a strict agenda.
e Ask the chair for permission to speak.

One person (often called the facilitator) usually takes notes while the others come up with ideas. Ideas are just noted down initially and they're not judged till later. Wild ideas are encouraged. While a strict agenda probably won't be followed, the facilitator may act to keep participants focused on the topic.

One conversation at a time is generally perceived as the best way of ensuring participants can build on the ideas of others.

2 [2.1] In this meeting people are brainstorming ideas for a baldness remedy. If you feel that this could be a sensitive topic for any of your students, you may prefer to do the extra activity on brainstorming on page 49.

Play the recording without stopping, and rewind if necessary for students to answer the question.

ANSWER
The product is a hair restorer and baldness remedy.

3 [2.1] See what questions students can answer from memory before playing the recording again. Pause where appropriate to collect the remaining answers.

ANSWERS
a She take notes.
b 'The product is exciting', 'what the product does', 'sex appeal', and 'information'
c Roberto is bald himself, and so a potential user of the product. Also, it seems she respects his views more than Peter's.
d executive names: Chief, Top Man, Boss Man.
  medical names: Zamtex, Follitex
  masculine names: Macho, Sportsman, Tarzan
e Hair Today

4 [2.1] The listening text contains many different suggestions. Tell the class to stop you every time they identify one as you play the recording again. Alternatively, allow students to look at the tapescript on page 64 of the Student's Book and underline suggestion phrases while they listen.

ANSWERS
I think we should call it Hair …
We'd better appoint someone …
Let's start with the message.
Shall we let Roberto finish?
How about trying to convey the idea of youth?
Why don't we look for an 'executive' name?
We could call it Chief …
Could we have a name that inspires confidence?
Why not something with a medical sound?
Is it a good idea to look for a masculine name?
I don't think we should criticize one another's ideas at this stage.
I think we should have a name that tells the consumer …
What about Hair Now?
I think we should call it: Hair Today.
We'd better not use that one.

Organize the students into groups of three or four to take parts and read the tapescript aloud.

5 This exercise checks students can use some common suggestion forms correctly.

Sharing ideas

ANSWERS
a *I think we should …* and *We'd better …*
b *How about …*
c *Is it a good idea …?* (Be ready to point out that *We'd better …* is not followed by a full infinitive.)
d *We'd better not …;* and *had*
e *I think we shouldn't …* and *I don't think we should …* (more common); *Do you think we should …?*

EXTRA ACTIVITY
Check students can use some common expressions with prepositions correctly. Tell them to complete these sentences with gerunds (-ing forms).
e.g. When this lesson finishes, how about going for a drink?

1 *When this lesson finishes, how about …?*
2 *Everyone at work is talking about …*
3 *No company can make money without …*
4 *I need to check my calendar before …*
5 *I can save time on my journey to work by …*
6 *I'm starting a new business and I thought you might be interested in …*
7 *I'd like to stay in tonight instead of …*
8 *My boss is really good at …*
9 *I'm looking forward to …*

Students may offer noun phrases that are also possible, such as:
I'm looking forward to the conference.
If they do, accept their answers and point out that gerunds are nouns too. Encourage them to suggest answers with gerunds.
e.g. I'm looking forward to meeting you at the conference.

6 Students often lack phrases to indicate their responses to ideas, so spend some time getting your class to practise saying these phrases in different ways.

POSSIBLE ANSWERS
a positive
b negative
c both
d both
e positive
f both

When said with sarcastic intonation, even the positive responses here could sound negative.

7 These scenarios vary in urgency and degree of risk to provide opportunities for practising both forceful and more tentative suggestion forms. Encourage the students to use not only different suggestion forms, but also the different responses in **6**.

Task

Students normally decide to market this product to old people, students, or both groups. Their marketing plans will depend on their choice.

In large classes, allow time at the end for groups to report their ideas back to the whole class.

EXTRA ACTIVITY
*For further brainstorming practice, see **Activity 1** on page 49.*

GREAT INVENTIONS

The reading text in this section prepares students to discuss the benefits an innovation has brought to their workplace and the language focus is on the passive. While intermediate students should have little difficulty forming the passive, they are likely to have difficulties knowing when to use it and so that is the focus here.

1 Write the inventions the students suggest on the board.

2 Call on a student to read the first paragraph aloud to the class and ask everyone to suggest what the invention was. If they suggest 'fire', tell them to write it in the space provided. Continue in this manner to guess all the inventions, or instruct students to continue in pairs or small groups.

When you've finished, go back to the inventions the students suggested in **1** and see if they predicted any in the article. Ask the students which invention they think has had the greatest effect on modern life and why. Then look at File 2 on page 56 of the Student's Book to confirm answers.

3 Ask students to identify the active and passive forms individually or in pairs. Avoid making contrasts that involve transforming sentences from active to passive. While they may illustrate differences in form, they are not helpful for illustrating differences in use. It is more helpful to point to examples where the subject of the sentence stays the same.

e.g. *The printing press was invented by Guttenberg.* (Passive – the sentence is about what happened to the printing press.)

Sharing ideas

The printing press enabled people to mass produce books. (Active – the sentence is about what the printing press did.)

> **ANSWERS**
> The passive forms are:
> – they *are used* everywhere.
> – This *was invented* in Germany by Johannes Gutenburg around 1450.
> – It *was* even *described* as 'a solution looking for a problem'.
> – and since then, new forms *have been developed*
> – Without it, the more sophisticated technologies of TV, satellites, and cell phones might never *have been invented*.
> **a** We use active forms to describe what the inventions have done.
> **b** We use passive forms to describe what's happened to the inventions.
>
> Passives are common when we're thinking about what's done or what happens to something or someone, rather than what the thing or person does.

4 In this exercise, the opening sentence introduces the thing or device that the next sentences will be about, e.g. a new robot, pager, fan, etc. The sentence that follows adds more information about the thing or device. It either says what it does, or it says what's happened to it. If it's the former, the active form is more appropriate. If it's the latter, the passive form is more appropriate.

> **ANSWERS**
> a 2   d 2
> b 1   e 2
> c 1   f 1

5 This is an information gap activity. Monitor the activity giving individual help where appropriate, e.g. if a student doesn't know anything about an invention they have to explain. If students are unable to guess an invention, they should move on to the next one and come back later. If you wish, you can introduce an element of competition, so the first pair to finish are the winners.

Task

1 and **2** As in the Student's Book. Encourage students to ask one another questions about the innovations they describe.

EVALUATING IDEAS

The first exercises in this section focus attention on some simple but very common discourse markers we use to describe consequences. It's particularly useful for students who might overuse more formal words and expressions such as *therefore*, *leads to*, and *results in*, which are relatively uncommon in spoken English.

1 [2.2] Play the recording then discuss the questions with the whole class. If students are surprised by this proposal, point out that some notable companies such as Starbucks give shares, even to part-time employees.

2 [2.2] Play the recording again, pausing where necessary for students to complete the sentences.

> **ANSWERS**
> a so …   d It means …
> b That way …   e Then …
> c It's going to make …

3 Students can do this matching activity in pairs or individually.

> **ANSWERS**
> a 4   d 3
> b 1   e 2
> c 5

4 [2.3] Play the recording then ask students to discuss the question as a class or in pairs.

5 [2.3] Play the recording again pausing to allow the students to write down the second half of the sentences.

> **ANSWERS**
> **a** it'd dilute the value of our stock.
> **b** we'll have to find another way to deal with the problem.
> **1** *b* is possible (*if* + present simple + *will* + infinitive)
> **2** *a* is possible in theory but unlikely to happen in practice (*if* + simple past + *would* + infinitive)

Sharing ideas

Check students know:
- the *'ll* and *'d* contractions represent *will* and *would*.
- both these structures refer to future possibilities, even though sentence a contains a past tense form.

You may wish to refer students to the language notes on conditionals on pages 71–2.

6 Make sure students write *1* or *2* beside each prompt to enable you to check they are using the appropriate conditional form later.

7 Students do this exercise in pairs first. Then, go round the class collecting some of their sentences.

Quick check

This can be done before or after the Task.

> POSSIBLE ANSWERS
> 1 How do you feel about this?
>   What's your opinion on this?
>   What are your views on this?
> 2 What do you think about 'e-commerce'? (Give me your opinion.)
>   What does 'e-commerce' mean? (Explain the meaning of the word.)
>   What do you mean by 'e-commerce'? (Give me your interpretation of the meaning of the word.)
> 3 *I agree* is correct (and *I am agree* is wrong).
>   Do you agree?
>   I don't agree / I disagree.

In many languages *agree* can be an adjective as well as a verb. In English it is only a verb.

> EXTRA ACTIVITY
> *To check your students' pronunciation of numbers before they do the task, write these numbers on the board and ask students how they would say them.*
> 3 p.m.   three pee em
>   three o'clock (in the afternoon)
> £60,000   sixty thousand pounds
> $1,800   eighteen hundred dollars
>   one thousand eight hundred dollars
> 2/3   two thirds
> 8.43%   eight point four three per cent
> *If necessary, point out that:*
> – *we write the currency sign before a number, but say it after the number.*
> – *numbers in the low thousands might be pronounced differently.*

> $2,100   two thousand one hundred dollars
>   (British English)
>   twenty one hundred dollars
>   (US English)
> – *numbers are pronounced separately after a decimal point.*
> 18.18   eighteen point one eight

Task

Tell students to read the texts on their own, or ask some students to read the texts aloud. They then work in pairs or small groups to work through the questions. Allow time for students to report any interesting observations to the whole class.

> EXTRA ACTIVITIES
> 1 *See* **Activity** *2 on page 50 for a pairwork task that involves evaluating more business ideas.*
> 2 *For further practice of discourse markers to indicate consequences, play this variation of the traditional 'consequences' game:*
>
> *Each student needs a piece of paper and pen. (Teacher's might like to join in as well.) Students should begin by writing a suggestion starting:*
>
> I think we should ...
>
> *It can be any suggestion they wish, but you might like to encourage suggestions for improvements at work, e.g.* I think we should buy some new software. *If they have difficulty thinking of original ideas, allow them to use one they've just read about, e.g.* I think we should hold meetings standing up.
>
> *Then they fold the paper over so what they have written cannot be seen, and pass it on to the person sitting to their right. On the next piece of paper, they should then write:* So ..., *and give a reason for their suggestion.*
>
> *They fold over the paper again, pass it on and write:* That way..., *and continue with what will follow from that.*
>
> *And so it goes on in the same way with:* It's going to make ..., It means ..., *and* Then ...
>
> *The papers are then opened up and read out to the class.*

Sharing ideas

MANAGING DISCUSSIONS

Students often feel more confident about participating in English meetings when they are equipped with common phrases for discussions. This section will equip them with a list of such phrases, as well as raising awareness of the skills they will need to manage discussions.

> *EXTRA ACTIVITY*
> *See Activity 3 on page 51 for further discussion of students' linguistic needs for meetings.*

1 Discuss these questions with the whole class. Make a note on the board of students' suggestions of tasks that a chairperson needs to perform, so that you'll be able to refer to them in **2**.

2 **2.4** Play the recording through, pausing after each section to collect answers.

> ANSWERS
> The chair perfoms all the tasks listed later in **3**. Opinions may vary, but probably the chair performs quite well under difficult circumstances.

3 Students can perform this matching activity individually or in pairs. Check answers with the whole class.

> ANSWERS
> a 3   d 7   g 4
> b 5   e 1   h 2
> c 8   f 9   i 6

4 **2.4** Before you play the recording, instruct students to stop you when they hear one of the expressions. Alternatively, play the recording and instruct students to follow in the tapescript on page 65 and to underline the expressions.

5 Explain that multiword verbs are very common in spoken English. Warn students that it's often not possible to guess their meanings by looking at them. They need to be learnt as vocabulary items. The multiword verbs in this exercise are recycled elsewhere in the Student's Book.

> ANSWERS
> a continue   e go faster
> b consider   f cause
> c discuss   g handle
> d delay   h rely on

You may wish to organize the students into groups of four to take parts and read the tapescript aloud.

Task

As in the Student's Book.

HOLDING A MEETING

This task is the culminating challenge of this unit. It will involve brainstorming, drawing up a meeting agenda, problem solving, and discussion skills.

1 Write the students' suggestions on the board and encourage wild whacky answers before reading the text.

2 In small classes this can be done as a whole class activity, with notes made on the board. In large classes, ensure someone is appointed to take notes in each group, then call on them to report some of the ideas back to the class.

3 The students will have already thought of some of these ideas, or variations on them. There may be other ideas here though that they can add to their own lists.

4 The students should use their lists to write the agenda. Instruct them to assign different topics and proposals to different group members. Everyone should be responsible for introducing the discussion of at least one idea.

5 The decision about whether the meeting should be chaired or not is probably best left to your class and either alternative is equally valid. Some students frequently attend formal chaired meetings while others attend informal unchaired meetings. If necessary, point out that in meetings with no chairperson, students share a joint responsibility for ensuring everyone's views are collected and discussed.

6 As in the Student's Book. At the end, you and your students can evaluate the meeting in terms of how successful it was in terms of:

- coming up with effective solutions
- coming up with original solutions
- covering the agenda
- gathering everyone's views and achieving consensus
- organizing what's to be done and who's to do it.

Sharing ideas

3 Tackling problems

Language work

The six sections of this unit look at:
- Present perfect
- *should have done*
- Promising action
- Past tenses: simple, continuous, and perfect
- Modal verbs expressing obligation and possibility
- Making appointments
- Requests, offers, and invitations
- Telephone expressions
- Indirect questions

REPORTING PROBLEMS

For many students, the key context in which they have to make calls in English is to deal with problems. This section focuses attention on the perfect aspect of the verb in the context of both the present perfect tense, and *should have done*.

1 Discuss these questions with the whole class.

2 [3.1] Tell students they will only hear Gary's side of the conversation in this telephone call. If necessary play the recording twice to check students understand the problem fully.

> **ANSWER**
> The problem concerns the way some brake pads are being packed. The brake pads are difficult to remove from pallets and the problem has arisen in the last two weeks.

3 Students work in pairs to write down their suggested answers. Call on some students to read them out to the class. Accept all answers and don't confirm or correct at this stage.

4 [3.2] Allow them to correct their ideas of what Debbie said while they listen to the whole conversation. If necessary, pause after Debbie speaks. Check they have noted her questions and the promises she made correctly.

> **EXTRA ACTIVITY**
> Give students copies of Debbie's part and ask them to recall what Gary said.
> Debbie Hobbs.
> ......
> Hey Gary. How's it going?
> .....
> What's that?
> .....
> Don't they work?
> ...
> How long has this been going on?
> .....
> Of course. I'll look into it right away.
> ...
> What time is it there now?
> .....
> Then I'll try to get a quick answer. Which hotel are you in?
> ....
> OK, leave it with me. I'll take care of it.

Students can be instructed to work in pairs to recall the whole dialogue. One works with the tapescript on page 65 and the other works with their book closed. They then act out the call, with the person reading the tapescript prompting their partner when they need help.

5 Students can do this individually or in pairs.

> **ANSWERS**
> a 5   d 4
> b 2   e 3
> c 1

> **EXTRA ACTIVITIES**
> 1 Tell students to change the promises they have made in 5 into requests, e.g.:
>
>   Can you find out what's going on for me?
>   Will you get back to me?
>   Can you let me know?
>   Could you take care of it?
>   Would you look into it and work something out?
>
>   (There is more practice of request forms later in this unit in the section on Making arrangements.)

Tackling problems

21

> *2 Check students know the meaning of some other multiword verbs with* look. *Write these examples on the board:*
>
> look into   look after   look for
> look forward   to look something up
> look through
>
> *Read the sentences below and ask them to use one of these verbs to reformulate them, e.g.:*
> I'll investigate it. → I'll look into it.
>
> 1 *We're always seeking new business partners.* (We're always looking for new business partners.)
> 2 *I'm not sure what it means but I'll consult the dictionary.* (I'm not sure what it means but I'll look it up.)
> 3 *Quickly read these notes before the meeting.* (Look through these notes before the meeting.)
> 4 *Next time you're in town, pay us a brief visit.* (Next time you're in town, look us up.)
> 5 *We expect to hear from you shortly.* (We look forward to hearing from you shortly.)
> 6 *Who's taking care of this while John's away?* (Who's looking after this while John's away?)

6 🔊 3.3   Read through the questions, then play the recording.

> **ANSWERS**
> a They changed the stacking method in order to get more brake pads on each pallet and save money on shipping costs.
> b They should have checked with the customer before they changed it.
> c Debbie has told Logistics to change back to the old system for the time being. She has also arranged a meeting for when Gary returns.

Ask students if they have ever encountered problems similar to this in their jobs.

7 This exercise contrasts the use of the simple past and present perfect. Work through the questions with the whole class.

> **ANSWERS**
> Debbie's choice of tense here depends on her attitude to the past action. She uses:
> a the simple past when she's interested in what happened in the past.
> b the present perfect when she's interested in the current results of a past action.
> Logistics didn't check with the customer. When Gary say's 'first' he means, before they changed the packing system.

Draw attention to the similarities between the *have done* and *should have done* forms here. Point out that we use perfect verb forms when we see the time of an event as being earlier than some other time or event. Debbie set up a meeting and persuaded Logistics to revert back to the old system earlier and Gary thinks the customer should have been told earlier.

8 As in the Student's Book. Give students a minute or two to think about this before they talk to their partner.

Task

As in the Student's Book. Make sure students take time to read the role cards carefully and to think about what they might have to say in the calls.

> *EXTRA ACTIVITIES*
> 1 *Ask students what sort of problems they have to report or deal with over the phone in their jobs. Tell them to describe a typical problem and what happens in detail to a partner, then instruct them to act out the calls they make with the partner.*
> 2 *For further practice of the present perfect and* should have done, *use the statements in Activity 1 on page 52. Cut the page into separate boxes. Explain that there are three sentences/clauses: one about what's happened, one about the effects, and one about what should have happened, e.g.:*
>
>   – We changed our packing system …
>   – and a customer has complained.
>   – We should have checked with them before we made the change.
>
> *In small classes, put all the statements on a table and tell students to group them. In large classes, make it a mingling activity. Give students a box each and tell them to circulate to find their partners.*

Tackling problems

FINDING SOLUTIONS

The focus of this section is storytelling. Students will read a story, extract a moral, and then move on to tell their own stories.

1 As in the Student's Book. Accept any morals your students may suggest. Do not confirm or disallow any at this stage.

Students may like to know that the writer of this story, Peter Guber, was the Chairman and CEO of Sony Pictures Entertainment from 1989 to 1995. The movies that he helped to produce there earned more than $3 billion worldwide and received more than 50 Academy Award nominations. In 1995 he founded Mandalay, which has made such films as *Donnie Brasco* with Al Pacino and Johnny Depp, and *Seven Years in Tibet* with Brad Pitt. Sigourney Weaver starred in *Gorillas in the Mist*.

2 As in the Student's Book.

> **ANSWERS**
> a A very high altitude, jungle location, Rwanda was on the verge of revolution, and they needed more than 200 animals.
> b The studio thought they would exceed the budget.
> c The story required the gorillas to 'act'.
> d He sent a cinematographer into the jungle to film the gorillas and they created a story around the shots he took.

3 Discuss this as a class before students read the final part of Peter Guber's story in File 7 on page 58 of the Student's Book.

4 This exercise contrasts three different past tense forms.

> **ANSWERS**
> happened – simple past
> was producing – past continuous
> asked – simple past
> had meant – past perfect
> a The past perfect is used to show one event happened before another in the past.
> b The past continuous is used to set the scene and describe the circumstances of a past event.
>
> Other examples from the story:
>
> *had become a nightmare* – past perfect
> *was financing the movie* – past continuous
> *what she was doing* – past continuous

5 Students complete this individually, then check their answers with a partner.

> **ANSWERS**
> 1 learned/learnt
> 2 was making
> 3 included
> 4 involved
> 5 was talking
> 6 was
> 7 saw
> 8 had approved/approved
> 9 had selected/selected
> 10 added up/was adding up
> 11 had made/made
> 12 had made/made

Task

As in the Student's Book.

If students are short of ideas, suggest that they might have stories to do with:

- a person who taught them a lot
- a problem they once faced at work
- a training course they have taken
- mistakes they have made
- mistakes other people have made.

> *EXTRA ACTIVITY*
> *Joke telling provides a natural way to practise past tenses. Here's one you can tell to get your class started telling jokes that they know:*
> *This is a story about a shepherd who lived on a peaceful mountain far away. One day he was watching his sheep when suddenly a brand new Range Rover came driving up the mountain towards him, going very fast and making lots of noise. The driver was a young man wearing an Armani suit, with Gucci shoes, RayBan sunglasses and a Hermes tie. He leaned out of the window and asked the shepherd: 'If I can tell you exactly how many sheep you have in your flock, will you give me one?' The shepherd looked at the young man, then he looked at his sheep and calmly answered, 'Sure!' The young man parked the car, took out his laptop computer, connected it to a cell-phone, surfed to a NASA page on the Internet and called up a GPS satellite navigation system. In just one minute, he had scanned the area, opened up a database and 30 Excel spreadsheets with complex formulae. Then he printed out a 10-page*

Tackling problems

report on his hi-tech miniaturized printer, turned round to the shepherd and said: 'You have exactly 1,498 sheep!' 'That's correct,' said the shepherd. 'You can take one'. After the young man had chosen a sheep and put it into his Range Rover, the shepherd asked, 'If I can tell you exactly what your business is, will you give me my sheep back?' 'Okay, why not?' the young man said. 'You are a consultant,' said the shepherd. 'That's correct,' replied the young man, 'but how did you know?' 'Easy,' said the shepherd. 'You turned up here although nobody called you. You wanted to be paid for the answer to a question I already knew the answer to. And you don't know a damn thing about my business because you took my dog.'

STAFFING PROBLEMS

This section builds up to students holding a meeting to solve a difficult staff retention problem.

1 Discuss the questions with the whole class. If students suggest benefits are important for retaining employees, take the opportunity to teach the more informal term *perks*. If appropriate, draw attention to the collocations in the instructions: *to fill a job, to keep good employees,* and ask students to think of similar expressions, e.g. *to fill a position/post, to retain good employees*.

> Note: In American English, the term *turnover* refers to *staff turnover* – the rate at which employees join and leave a company. In British English, it can have this meaning too, but *turnover* is also used in the UK to describe *revenues* – the amount of money a company receives from sales in a given period, usually twelve months.

2 Read the introduction to the text with the whole class and make sure students understand what *recognition* and *be promoted* mean. (These words will be important when they come to the final task.) The rest of the text can be read individually, in pairs, or as a whole class activity. Find out which benefits students would like most and why.

3 Ensure students use appropriate modal verbs when you collect their answers.

ANSWERS
a Because labour is in short supply, and good benefits help attract and keep staff.
b They can take a nap on a futon (a Japanese sleeping mattress) or have a massage.
c They have to get married.
d You should try to work for Nokia because it will reimburse some of your tuition costs.
e You must wear *something* to work. You mustn't go naked! You don't have to wear smart clothes.
f Students' own answers.

4 Point out that modal verbs add extra meaning to other verbs to show the speaker's attitude or opinion. The modals in these exercises all express obligation, necessity, or ability. (Modal verbs used to express possibility and certainty will be practised in the next unit.)

ANSWERS
a need to, have got to, should, has to, must
b don't need to, don't have to
c can

5 Students can work in pairs or as a whole class.

ANSWERS
Very strong obligation: *must, have got to, have to*
Strong obligation: *need to*
Weak obligation: *should, ought to*

The negative forms are:
don't have to, must not, shouldn't, ought not to, don't need to, haven't got to
Must not can be contracted to *mustn't* in British English.

a verbs we use to talk about things that are forbidden or prohibited:
 must not, shouldn't, ought not to
b verbs we use to talk about things that aren't necessary:
 don't have to, don't need to, haven't got to

In many languages, the context indicates whether the negative form implies lack of obligation or prohibition. This is not the case in English and students may be surprised. Make sure they understand the difference. If necessary refer students to the language notes on modals on page 71.

Students may ask when we use *must* and *have to*. *Have to* is used more commonly than *must* in both British and American English, but *must* is rarely used

Tackling problems

in American. In British English we tend to use *must* when we are talking about what the speakers or listeners want.

You must stop me if I'm speaking too fast.
I must remember to ask for a receipt before we leave.

We tend to use *have to* when there is some sort of external obligation.

All employees have to wear a suit and tie.
We have to show our receipts to claim our expenses.

6 Students can work in pairs or small groups.

7 Discuss this with the whole class.

Task

In some countries, the term *staff* applies only to a certain group of employees, generally an executive level support group, in an organization. If necessary, check students understand that in English *staff* can refer to all the employees of a company.

These statistics here are taken from the results of a survey by Reed Personnel Services, a leading recruitment specialist in the UK. It surveyed over 400 organizations to assess attitudes to staff turnover and to investigate staff retention policies in these organizations.

1 Allow students time to study the statistics before leading a whole class discussion of the questions.

2 and **3** Students can prepare their ideas individually or in pairs. In large classes at the end of the meetings, call on different groups to present their solutions to the class.

You might want to evaluate the presentations in terms of:

- how clear and comprehensive the solutions were
- how creative the solutions were
- how practical the solutions were.

CHANGING PLANS

In addition to practising some common expressions for making arrangements, this section provides opportunities to raise students' awareness of differences in register.

1 Invite answers from the whole class. You could also ask if telephone calls in English cause them any difficulties and, if so, what sort of difficulties.

Quick check

POSSIBLE ANSWERS

1
a Hold on.
One moment, please.
Just a second, please.
Bear with me a moment, please.
b I'm afraid Mrs Clark is …
not available/out of the office today/ in a meeting/on the other line/on vacation this week
c Are you busy?
Is this a good time to call?
Am I calling at a bad/inconvenient time?
d I think that's everything …
Is there anything else?
Anyway …
OK …
Right then …
e It's been great talking to you.
Thanks for calling.
Take care now.

2
a	M, O, etc.	f	s, c, etc.
b	-	g	:
c	_	h	/
d	47	i	22
e	@	j	.

These messages contain several examples of things that commonly cause difficulties when dictating information over the phone. Useful expressions you might want to provide are:

Mc – that's an upper case M and a lower case c
The country code is …
…, that's the area code.
ö – an 'o' with two dots on the top
å – an 'a' with a little circle on top (Take this opportunity to check any letters from your students' languages that don't appear in the English alphabet.)
at hotmail dot com
usa dot org

We generally pronounce the suffixes *com, net,* and *org* as if they were one word, but letters are pronounced separately in the suffixes *ac, edu,* and *tv.*
Students may ask about the slash (/). This is generally called a *slash,* or *forward slash.*

Tackling problems

25

2 [3.4] Students listen and take notes while they listen.

ANSWER
Callers have three alternatives. They can:
- press the star key on their telephones which will enable them to send their telephone number to the screen of Peter Clark's pager.
- call Peter on his cell phone: 202 555 7639
- record a message and wait for Peter to return their call.

Note: In British English a cell phone is called a mobile (phone).

3 While students deliver their voicemail messages, ask other members of the class to note them down. Ensure your students pronounce their telephone numbers clearly in their messages. In British and American English we normally pronounce telephone numbers as individual numbers and pause after three, four, or even five numbers (not two). There are a few exceptions to this with numbers containing several zeros, e.g.:

1800 555 2000 = *one eight hundred, five five five, two thousand*

4 [3.5] As in the Student's Book.

POSSIBLE ANSWERS
Caller: Carmen Santez
Message: She can't make Friday's meeting because she has to go back to Argentina earlier than planned.
Contact details: The Marriot Marquis Hotel – 212 398 1900 – Room 1147.

5 [3.6] Students can work in pairs, or you may wish to do the following:

Write individual phrases from the conversation on separate pieces of paper. In large classes, distribute them to individual students and instruct them to arrange themselves into a line in the correct order. In small classes, allow students to rearrange the slips of paper in order on a table.

After students have written numbers in the boxes, get them to read the conversation in pairs and make any necessary corrections before playing the recording.

ANSWERS
1, 6, 2, 7, 10, 8, 4, 3, 9, 5, 11

6 Collect suggestions for alternative phrases from the whole class and write them on the board for students to copy.

POSSIBLE ANSWERS
a I'm sorry but I can't come to Friday's meeting.
  I'm afraid something's come up and I can't get to our meeting on Friday.
b What time suits you?
  When is good for you?
  When are you free?
c How about Tuesday afternoon?
  Is Tuesday afternoon OK/convenient/good for you?
  Are you free on Tuesday afternoon?
  Does Tuesday afternoon suit you?
d That suits me.
  That's great.

7 As in the Student's Book.

ANSWERS
a 3   c 4
b 2   d 1

Explain that the level of formality of the request form we choose usually depends on two factors:

- how well we know the person we're speaking to
- the size of the request.

Then collect alternative phrases, write them on the board and ask students to grade them in terms of formality. Also collect replies for saying *yes* and saying *no*. Below is a list of possible alternatives.

Asking people to do things for us:
…., will you?
Can you …?
Could you …?
Would you …?
*Would you mind … (-ing)?
Draw attention to the fact that *Would you mind …?* is followed by a gerund (-*ing* form).
Saying *yes*:   Saying *no*:
Sure.   I'm afraid …
Yes, certainly.   I'm sorry, but …
Of course.
*Not at all.

Tackling problems

Asking for permission to do things ourselves:
Can I …?
Could I …?
May I …?
*Do you mind if I …?

Saying *yes*:   Saying *no*:
Yes of course.   I'm afraid …
Sure, go ahead.   I'm sorry, but …
Please do.
*Not, at all.

Inviting people to do things with us:
Do you want to …?
Would you like to …?

Saying *yes*:   Saying *no*:
Yes please. I'd like that.   I'm afraid …
Thank you. That'd be great.   I'd love to but …
                                  I'd rather not, if that's OK.

Offering to do things for other people:
Shall I …?
Do you want me to …?
Would you like me to …?

Saying *yes*:   Saying *no*:
Thank you very much   No, it's all right thanks.
Yes please. That'd be great.   That's very kind of you but I
                                 can manage.

*Check the class can answer requests with *mind* correctly by making some requests to students yourself, e.g.:
You: Do you mind if I borrow your dictionary?
Student: No, go ahead.
You: Would you mind lending me your pen?
Student: Not at all. (ie. I am happy to lend it.)
Explain *mind* means *object to* and so a negative answer indicates agreement to a request.

> EXTRA ACTIVITY
> *For further practice of these polite forms, give students the mini role-plays in **Activity 2** on page 53. Cut the cards out and distribute them. Students take turns to make the requests and offers.*

8 As in the Student's Book.

Task

Allow students a short time to read their role cards and to think about what they might need to say before each of the calls. Simulate a phone call by seating pairs of students back to back so they cannot see one another. Alternatively, if resources permit, get pairs of students to use real phones to make the calls.

Call 1
Gather all the students who will be playing the role of B (the students with the information at the back of the book) together. Out of earshot of the As, make sure they realise that they should not play the role of a human being in this call. They are simply a recorded message, so they should not reply to their partner.

Call 2
As in the Student's Book.

Call 3
There is no time when both students have a clear space in their diaries. One of them could offer to cancel another arrangement, but the best solution is probably to arrange the visit for Thursday. A's car will be at the garage, but they may be able to arrange alternative transport.

> EXTRA ACTIVITY
> *Students who need to write English letters, faxes or e-mails will appreciate **Activity 3** on correspondence on page 54.*
>
> **Answers**
> 2 1 **have** to agree
>   2 **Don't make** sentences …
>   3 commas that are not …
>   4 **its** proper place … **it's** not needed
>   5 Don't repeat yourself
>   6 Always check your spelling
>   7 if you **missed** any words out
>
> 3 a 3, b 4, c 7, d 1, e 6, f 8, g 5, h 2

COMPLAINTS

In this section students listen to two different versions of the same conversation in which someone makes a complaint. The linguistic differences between the two conversations are very subtle, but have a huge impact on the outcome of the call.

1 Discuss these questions with the whole class. They set the scene for the conversation students will hear in **2**.

2 3.7 Tell students to close their books and listen, then ask them what the problem was.

Tackling problems

> **ANSWER**
> The customer has been overcharged. She rented a car in Las Vegas for four hours and her credit card has been billed for four days.

3 ▢ Play the recording two or three times, pausing where necessary to collect all the answers.

> **ANSWERS**
> a Because she has wasted half an hour trying to get through the car rental agency's automated telephone answering system. (Check your students understand this is a menu system which plays recorded messages and directs calls.)
> b Because the agent was silent. Presumably the agent was looking the details up on their computer system, but the caller couldn't see that.
> c Because it was a Sunday so the office had shut early.
> d Because she left Las Vegas the next day (Monday).
> e Because there are no supervisors – (just a team).

4 Students can read through the conversation in pairs before answering the questions. Make sure they become familiar with this conversation. They are going to hear a different version of it in **5**, which has a successful outcome. The linguistic differences are subtle, and the better they know this first conversation, the better they will be able to appreciate the differences.

> **ANSWERS**
> Students' own answers, and they may disagree about who is most at fault here. Encourage discussion and avoid confirming or refuting answers at this stage.

5 ▢ Tell students to close their books and listen to the second version of the conversation. Establish that the outcome was more successful and ask why. Students won't be able to answer fully until they examine the differences between the calls in detail.

> **POSSIBLE REASONS**
> 1 The agent diffused the customer's anger at the delay in answering by apologizing.
> 2 The customer didn't blame the agent directly for the mistake.
> 3 The agent remembered the location of the hire.
> 4 The agent explained to the customer that she was calling up information on her screen.
> 5 The agent stated that there was a problem, without implying the customer was lying.
> 6 The customer offered proof that she had left Las Vegas on the Monday.

6 ▢ Play the recording, pausing when necessary so students can pencil the differences onto the script.

> **ANSWERS**
> See tapescript and items listed in **5** above.

7 ▢ and **8** ▢ Students should write 'more courteous' versions of the dialogues in pairs. Once you've corrected them, ask pairs of students to act them out to the class, before playing the recording.

Task

Before beginning, check students understand the difference between interpreting services (providing simultaneous spoken translations of what people say) and translating services (translating written documents). Make sure they have enough time to read the handwritten notes on their copies of the invoice.

> **EXTRA ACTIVITIES**
> *1 Give students who made the complaints the chance to deal with complaints instead, and vice versa. Tell the class that the person who went on the business trip paid Eloquencia the sums they agreed on the phone. However, when their boss saw the bill, they complained about all the extra charges.*
>
> *Tell them to act out another call. The person who complained to Eloquencia in the last call will keep the same role. But this time they will receive a call from their boss who is going to complain about the invoice. (The person who owned Eloquencia in the last call becomes the boss.)*

Tackling problems

> 2 For many students, time pressure is a big issue on the telephone. Being able to employ phrases that buy time such as 'I'm just calling it up on my screen' can be very helpful. For further practice of such phrases and of operating under time pressure on the phone, see **Activity 4** on pages 55 and 56.
>
> This extra activity is a pairwork task in which students have different roles. Half the class will need a copy of page 55 and the other half will need a copy of page 56. The answers to the questions all appear in different sections of the Student's Book, so they will need to have this to hand.

Quick check

Check students understand that indirect questions:

- are polite forms
- are generally used to get information at the start of conversations
- don't contain auxiliary verbs
- contain 'if' or 'whether' if their answer is *yes* or *no*.

> **ANSWERS**
> Could you tell me/Do you know …
> **a** what time the banks close?
> **b** where the nearest chemist is?
> **c** if this bus goes to Terminal 4?
> **d** what time the restaurant opens?
> **e** how I get to the city centre from here?
> **f** whether there's an Internet café near here?

GOING PLACES

This game revises language practised in all of the earlier sections in this unit. It can be played in pairs, or students can form small teams that compete against one another. All that's needed is a coin.

Pre-teach the following:

to toss a coin
heads
tails
It's your go.
Is it my turn?

If necessary, show the class how to play the game by demonstrating with two students. Where, for example, students are given an instruction such as 'call room service and order a meal', their partner should play the role of the hotel staff.

Tackling problems

4 Planning ahead

Language work

The five sections of this unit look at:
- Expressions for talking about the future
- Modal verbs and expressions of probability and possibility
- Adjectives – connotations, compounds, and antonyms
- *if, when, unless, in case, until*
- verb-noun collocations

PRESENTING PLANS

This section provides valuable practice in discussing plans and budgets. It aims to remind students of the wide variety of forms and expressions they can employ to do this.

1 Discuss these questions with the whole class. Suggestions might include: solar power, power from fossil fuels, nuclear power, wind power, hydro-electric power, etc.

2 Ask students to look at the picture then discuss this as a whole class.

3 [4.1] Write the questions students predict on the board so you can compare them later with the questions on the recording. You may wish to suggest students read through the vocabulary before you play the recording to give them more help.

4 [4.1] Play the recording again, pausing when necessary to collect answers.

> **ANSWERS**
> a False (Though he sounds evasive so he may be lying.)
> b True
> c False (The maximum number is 22.)
> d False (Though they will only be visible from the highest point of Logan Road.)
> e True
> f True
> g False (5,000 homes)
> h True

5 [4.1] This text contains many different verbs and phrases that we commonly use to express our thoughts about the future. The goal here is to help your students to identify them and discuss them. Demonstrate the sorts of words and phrases you're looking for first if necessary by playing the start of the recording and collecting the first few as a whole class activity. After that, you can:

- instruct students to stop you every time they hear a verb or expression that expresses a thought about the future
- hand over the tape recorder controls to a student and let them stop it instead (particularly useful in one to one classes)
- allow students to read the tapescript on pages 66–7 while listening, and instruct them to underline all the verbs and phrases instead.

When the class has identified the verbs and expressions, ask them to try to categorize them in terms of whether they describe:

a feelings about the future, e.g. *want*
b intentions, e.g. *plan*
c how certain the speaker feels. e.g. *doubt*
d when something will happen.

There are no tidy answers to these questions, as many verbs and expressions convey a mixture of these things, but this is an opportunity for you to raise awareness of the variety of future verbs.

> **POSSIBLE ANSWERS** (in the same order as they occur in the recording)
>
> *(be) about to* (when something will happen, i.e. very soon)
> *want to* (a feeling about the future – desire)
> *expect* (fairly certain)
> *will* (certain)
> *would you like to* (a feeling about the future – desire)
> *planning to* (an intention)
> *won't* (certain something isn't going to happen)
> *intending* (an intention)
> *going to* (an intention or certainty that something will happen)
> *aiming to* (an intention and possibly a desire as well)
> *estimate* (fairly certain)
> *look forward to* (a feeling about the future – desire, and also fairly certain)
> *we're due to* (when something will happen and possibly fairly certain)
> *doubt* (not certain)

EXTRA DISCUSSION POINT
In some cultures, speakers tend to express quantities very precisely, particularly in business presentations, e.g. thirty-six point eight three nine four percent. If you feel it is appropriate, draw attention to the vague expression of quantities in this part of the listening text:

We *estimate* 22 turbines will produce *around* 42 million kW hours a year. Now, an average house uses *roughly* 8,000 kW hours. So if we go ahead, we can look forward to enough electricity for *about* 5,000 homes.

Point out that such vagueness is common in English, even in scientific discussions where the speakers know the exact quantities, and not to use these expressions could sound strange.

6 As in the Student's Book.

Task

1 Exploit the visual of loft insulation, a long-life bulb, and solar panels. Ask the whole class which products in the pictures they think are most effective in terms of saving energy and most cost effective in terms of return on investment. Encourage them to think of other ways to save energy and make brief notes of their ideas on the board.

2 and **3** In small classes, this can be done individually. In large classes, students can work in teams and make joint presentations. Votes can be taken at the end to decide:

- whose ideas were most likely to reduce energy bills
- whose presentation was most convincing
- whose ideas were most original.

PREDICTIONS

After a brief presentation of probability expressions, this section moves on to a gambling game where students will negotiate deals. Although the language of the negotiations is likely to be fairly basic, students will need to employ more complex forms to express probability to explain the reason for their trades.

1 Discuss these questions with the whole class.

EXTRA ACTIVITY
Tell students that you're going to read some predictions that Bill Gates made in 1999 about the future of PCs. They should listen and see if they agree. Read the predictions below to the class and check they understand the vocabulary (see below).

- *For most people, the PC will remain the primary computing tool. You'll still want a big screen and a keyboard.*
- *The PC will work in tandem with other cool devices. You'll be able to share your data – files, schedule, calendar, e-mail, address book, etc. – across different machines; you won't have to think about it. It'll be automatic.*
- *There will be a simpler user interface that adapts to your needs, with voice recognition and natural-language processing.*
- *The PC will morph into many new forms, such as book size 'tablet PCs'.*

cool   fashionable, popular
a device   something made or adapted for a particular use
in tandem   together, at the same time and in corresponding ways
an interface   the way a computer program accepts information from or provides it to a user
to morph   to change shape
natural-language processing   software which enables computers to interpret human language
primary   most important, main
voice recognition   identifying a voice

Then ask:
1 Are any of these things happening now?
2 Is Bill Gates right about the others?
3 Which of these innovations would be most useful to you?

2 Discuss the statements with the whole class and invite suggestions for alternative ways of saying the same things replacing the words in italics.

3 Students work individually or in pairs.

Planning ahead

ANSWERS
a are definitely going to – will certainly
b are likely to – are probably going to
c might – could
d probably won't – aren't likely to
e certainly aren't going to – definitely won't

4 Ask students to read through the predictions individually and decide how they feel about them first, then exchange their opinions with a partner.

Task

This is a listening and speaking task, rather than just a speaking task. In order to perform well in the game, students will need to understand a recording of the business news and then use the information to make logical predictions. Begin by finding out whether any of your students own shares or track investments. Then explain that in this game, they will need to select promising investments.

EXTRA ACTIVITY
If you wish to check that students are familiar with some language used to describe trends, use Activity 1 on page 57.

Tell students to supply the missing prepositions.

Answers
Graph 1: to
Graph 2: by
Point out that to indicates the point reached but by indicates the difference.

1 In large classes, forming lots of small teams of three or four students is a bit chaotic, but generally more fun. Teams should read the texts about the companies together. Check that they have understood all the vocabulary before asking them to predict which companies' shares will rise.

2 Before beginning the trading, make sure everyone knows:

- that there is no money in this game – they should barter
- how many shares they have available for trading. Students working in teams should work this out themselves. If they decide to separate, each team member should know how many shares in which company they can trade.
- that they must record their transactions in writing on the chart.

In large classes, you could ask teams to stand up and walk around, approaching other teams to negotiate with. At the end of the trade, call on a few students to tell you what trades their team made and why. If necessary, encourage them to use modals and other expressions of probability. Check everyone has written their current position correctly in the chart under 'Position after trade 1.'

3 **4.2** As in the Student's Book. If students have difficulty understanding the listening text, play the recording again, pausing to ask the questions below to help them:

a Who is Harrison Kincaid? (The CEO of Connect-X)
b What has Connect-X done this week? (Signed contracts with four major computer companies.)
c What happened in H2's market tests? (Hydrogen gas exploded and injured six drivers.)
d What is H2 doing about it? (Stopping further tests until further research is completed.)
e How did the clinical trials of Zumoxin go? (Badly – some patients had negative side effects.)
f What's happened to Virtware's sales? (They've rocketed since the launch of its downloadable pet.)
g What problem is this causing? (Customers can't access their web site.)

Students can predict what will happen to the four companies' shares, either as a whole class activity, or secretly, in their teams.

4 As in the Student's Book. Again, make sure students record their transactions. Ask students to explain what trades they made (or tried to make) and why.

5 **4.3** Tell students to make a note of the share price while they are listening.

ANSWERS
Connect-X: $300
Virtware: $200
Empraxo: $50
H2: $1

Students can work out the value of their portfolios from these share prices. Congratulate the winners and commiserate with the losers.

Planning ahead

STRATEGY

In this section, students will read two case studies and draw comparisons, before moving on to discuss the business dilemma they raise and to conduct a SWOT analysis.

SWOT stands for strengths, weaknesses, opportunities, and threats. A SWOT analysis is a useful business tool for examining the interaction between a particular business or product and its market.

1 Discuss the questions with the whole class.

2 As in Student's Book. Alternatively, if you think students may find the text difficult to read individually, the class can be divided into two groups, with one group reading one case study together, and the other group reading the other. When they have finished, pair students with someone from the other group to do **3**.

3 As in the Student's Book. When pairs have finished asking and answering the questions, go through them with the whole class, collecting and checking the answers for both case studies.

| POSSIBLE ANSWERS | |
Minimills (page 40)	PCs (page 60)
a Minimills, the mid-1960s	PCs, the 1980s
b traditional large-scale steel mills	minicomputers
c They could only produce low-quality steel.	They were mostly purchased by individuals to play games.
d Upgraded their products for their most profitable customers. (Were happy to lose the low-end customers.)	Invested in developing high-performance high margin-products with ever-increasing computing power.
e Yes, their share prices rose.	Yes, they were regarded as very well managed.
f Their market share fell to less than 50% of the total market. (Their large-scale technology means they have to operate with a cost disadvantage.)	Several went out of business and the rest were badly damaged. They couldn't establish a viable position in the new market.

OPTIONAL FURTHER READING ACTIVITY
Instruct students to read the case study their partner told them about and look for other similarities between the two cases.

4 Discuss the question about the meaning with the whole class, or ask students to do this in pairs and report their answers to the class.

ANSWERS
a low-end – negative – quality
b viable – positive – money
c dynamic – positive – speed
d insignificant – negative – size
e down-market – negative – quality
f large-scale – * positive – size
g fast-growth – positive – speed
h high-margin – positive – money

*Though generally positive in a business context, large-scale can also have negative connotations, e.g. large-scale devastation.

5 Point out that many English adjectives can be formed by joining words with a hyphen, e.g. *a price-competitive market*.

ANSWERS
a low-margin
b small-scale
c slow-growth
d poorly-managed or badly-managed
e high-end or top-end
f up-market
g low-quality or poor-quality
h ever-decreasing

6 Collect students' opinions before reading the text. If students have difficulties understanding the text, guide them by asking these questions:

a What three characteristics do 'disruptive technologies' have? (They do jobs worse than established technologies, they are cheaper, and they improve over time.)
b What dilemma do established companies have to face when disruptive technologies come on to the market? (They have to focus on their existing customers, and they have to develop the disruptive technology, but they can't do both.)

Students might be interested to know that Professor Clayton Christensen's research in this area was

Planning ahead

sparked by a desire to find out why a group of good, smart managers would make a decision that turned out to be a bad one. It led to the research question: 'What can cause smart people to make wrong decisions?'

7 Ask students to discuss the questions in pairs or small groups first. Then collect ideas of examples of other disruptive technologies and solutions to the problem from the whole class. Avoid confirming or rejecting ideas at this stage. Students can do this themselves when they read the text in File 16 on page 62 at the back of the book.

> *EXTRA ACTIVITY*
> *Check students' pronunciation of the words* strengths *and* threats *before you start the task. You may need to do some pronunciation work on the aspirated th sound /θ/ and /s/.*
>
> *When students make the /θ/ sound, their tongues should touch the back of their teeth. If this is hard, tell them to try putting their finger in front of their mouth and touching it with their tongue when they say /θ/. When they make the sound /s/, their tongue should not touch the top of their mouth or their teeth. Practise saying these words:*
>
> **assets, things, growth, threats, strengths**

Task

Some students may be familiar with SWOT analyses and some may not. If appropriate, as well as reading the explanatory note in the glossary of the Student's Book, explain that a SWOT analysis is helpful for examining both the internal and external environment of a company, product, or product range.

> *EXTRA ACTIVITY*
> *The task can be repeated from a more personal angle. Ask students to analyse themselves (their personal strengths, weakness, opportunities, and threats) and their skills, and plan their future career strategy.*

BACK-UP PLANS

This section will be of particular interest to students who are, or will be, engaged in project work.

1 Discuss the questions with the whole class.

2 [4.4] Students should write any alterations to the budget in their books while you play the recording. Ask if the managers would spend the same amount with the alterations. (The changes they discussed would mean going over budget by $15,000.)

ANSWERS

	Current	New
Design work	$70,000	$85,000
Content development	$250,000	$200,000
Graphics development	$50,000	$100,000
Technical implementation	$300,000	$300,000

3 [4.4] Play the recording again, pausing where necessary to collect answers.

ANSWERS
a True
b False – it's slightly ahead of schedule
c True
d False – they won't see the design until they see the demo tomorrow
e True
f False – he/she will prepare revised figures (now), in case management ask to see them
g False – more hits than planned will blow the budget (cause a large overspend)

4 [4.4] As in the Student's Book.

ANSWERS
1 schedule
2 pressure
3 track
4 when
5 unless
6 until
7 in case

5 and **6** These are collocation exercises. (For more information on teaching collocations see page 10.) Write the phrase: *to _____ a deadline* on the board and ask students to brainstorm as many verbs as they can think of to fill the gap. Then repeat with the phrases:

to _____ pressure
to _____ a schedule

ANSWERS
For **5**, see **6**
a 3
b 1
c 2 (Only use the article *a* with: *to keep to, to draw up, to follow,* and *to disrupt*, i.e. *to disrupt a schedule* but *to be on schedule*.)

Planning ahead

Quick check

ANSWERS

1. a *on time*: at the correct time, promptly; *in time*: not late
   b *on budget*: spending the planned amount; *within budget* – not spending more than planned
2. a falling behind schedule
   b underspending
   c cutting a budget in half
3. Some verbs that are commonly used with both *money* and *time*:
   spend, save, waste, invest, make, lose

Other verbs commonly used with money:
earn, pay, donate, borrow, lend, squander, count

Point out that the noun *budget* has two different meanings in English. It can mean money allocated for a task or it can mean a target that you try to reach. Ask which meaning it has here. (Money allocated.)

7 Make sure students can answer the questions in brackets. They highlight the differences in meaning between the different connectors and *if*.

ANSWERS

1. *When* they see the design – it's certain that they will see it.
   If they see the design – it's not certain that they will see it. Perhaps they will and perhaps they won't.
2. *Unless* they tell her to – she will follow instructions.
   If they tell her to – she won't follow instructions. (Point out that *unless* is similar in meaning to *if not*.)
3. *In case* they want to make changes – she will draw up the design now.
   If they want to make changes – she will draw up the design later, but only if they want her to. (Point out that we often use *in case* to talk about precautions that need to be taken now to avoid problems in the future.)
4. *Until* they tell her to – she will implement the changes, at the time they tell her to.
   If they tell her to – perhaps they will tell her to implement the changes and perhaps they won't. If they do, she'll refuse or ignore the instruction.

Some languages have one preposition, which is broadly equivalent in meaning to both *until* and *by*, so be ready to explain the difference if necessary.

We use *until* (or more informally, *till*) for situations that continue up to a certain moment.

e.g. *I'll wait here till 4 p.m.* (I'm leaving at 4 p.m.)

We use *by* to say something will happen at or before a point in time in the future.

My colleague will be here by 4 p.m. (They may arrive before, but when it's 4 p.m. they will be here.)

8 Collect as many examples as you can from the class and write the best ones on the board. In order to check their use of tenses with these words, encourage students to use verbs where possible.

e.g. *I can't go home until I've finished my work* rather than *I can't go home until 4 o'clock*.

Point out that we often use a present tense to express a future idea, e.g.:

*I can't go home until my colleague **arrives**.*
*I'm going to retire when I **am** 60.*

These sentences are similar to first conditional forms in that we only rarely use *will* in the same clause as *if*.

Task

1, 2, and **3** As in the Student's Book. If you wish, a linguistic game element can be added to **3**. Students can score points for the correct use of connectors as follows:

When: 1 point
Unless: 2 points
Until or *till*: 2 points
In case: 3 points

Their partner should keep score and the student with the most points at the end wins.

> **EXTRA ACTIVITY**
> *Students involved in arranging schedules for projects will appreciate **Activity 2** on pages 58 and 59. There is only one possible solution to the problem.*
>
> **ANSWER**
>
> | | Crew | Crew | Crew |
> |---|---|---|---|
> | 11 a.m. – 12 a.m. | Hospital fire | Environmental protest | Bank robbery |
> | 12 a.m. – 1 p.m. | | | |
> | 1 p.m. – 2 p.m. | | President's visit | |
> | 2 p.m. – 3 p.m. | | | |
> | 3 p.m. – 4 p.m. | | | Actress |
> | 4 p.m. – 5 p.m. | | | Fireman |
> | 5 p.m. – 6 p.m. | | | Chocolate factory |

Planning ahead

NEW VENTURES

This unit culminates in a challenging task where students prepare a business plan for a new venture and present it to potential investors.

1 Discuss the questions with the whole class.

2 Read the advice for entrepreneurs together with the whole class and collect opinions before instructing students to read the interview text individually or in pairs. When they have read the interview, go back to the advice for entrepreneurs. Ask students whether they think Fred Abrew would agree with each one and why/why not.

> **POSSIBLE ANSWERS**
> *Work 7 days a week* … He probably agrees, because he is working harder than ever.
> *Treat your employees well.* Don't know because he doesn't mention this.
> *Buy low, sell high* … Don't know because doesn't mention this.
> *Listen carefully to your customers.* He agrees.
> *Do what you believe in* … He agrees. (He says he's having a ball.)
> *Use your contacts* … Don't know because doesn't mention this.
> *Learn from your mistakes* … He agrees.
> *Look for wealthy* … Don't know because doesn't mention this.

3 Students should refer back to the interview to find the answers to these questions.

> **ANSWERS**
> a He was the President of Equitable Resources Inc, a public utility company.
> b It provides e-business services and software tools to energy companies.
> c He saw that executives in the industry he worked in (the energy industry) were not exploiting technology and it was an opportunity.
> d It evaluated different energy companies' websites, compared their performance, and allowed them to read their results.
> e For EnergyE-comm.com it might have been gaining brand recognition, or spotting mistakes and correcting them fast. For Fred it was probably learning the technology.

4 In large classes, the best way to do this is to ask students to stand up and walk around to find people to form teams with. It's OK to have teams of different sizes.

Students can sit down and work with their books open going through the questions. Alternatively, you might like to instruct them to close their books and read the questions out yourself, one at a time, allowing time for discussion after each one.

5 Make sure that students know that their task here is to prepare a team presentation of their business plan. Every team member should make part of the presentation, and they can decide who will present what among themselves. The questions in **4** can be used as a guide for what to include. In very small classes, you may wish students to make individual presentations.

6 As in the Student's Book.

Instead of voting on the best business idea, you could hold votes on:

- which team had the most unusual/most viable/ best thought out business idea
- which team made the most professional/ persuasive/funniest presentation.

> **EXTRA ACTIVITY**
> *1 Tell students their companies have been operating for several years and they are very successful – so successful that a top business magazine would like to interview them. They should brainstorm some of the questions the interviewer could ask (they can refer back to the Fred Abrew text for ideas), and then act out the interviews in pairs.*
> *2 For further practice of some common verb-noun collocations that appear in this unit, play the domino game in Activity 3 on page 60. Cut out the 16 dominoes and distribute a full set to pairs or small groups of students. The game is played like the traditional game of dominoes. Students take it in turns to lay dominoes, but they can only connect words that commonly appear together. The first student to lay all their dominoes is the winner. When they have finished the game, they might like to try to form a continuous circle of dominoes.*

Planning ahead

5 Resolving conflict

Language work

The five sections of this unit look at:
- Direct and indirect language
- British and American English
- 2nd and 3rd conditional forms
- Verbs followed by gerunds and infinitives
- Negotiation expressions
- Adjectives ending in *-ed* and *-ing*

DROPPING HINTS

The language focus of this first section of the unit is concerned with pragmatics rather than grammar or vocabulary. The goal is to raise awareness that the meanings words convey may not be their literal meanings, and that often, more gets communicated than is actually said.

1 [5.1] Ask what *hint* means and if necessary explain it means suggesting something in an indirect way. Teach the expression 'to drop a hint'. Use the cartoon as an example.

ANSWERS
1 Those chocolates look nice. (I want to have one.)
2 You said you'd be here by eight. (You're late!)
3 Are you busy? (Can you do me a favour?)
4 Is anybody else feeling hot? (I'm hot.)
5 Goodness, is that the time? (I must leave).
6 Is that your car in my parking space? (Move your car out of my parking space.)
7 I thought I put a cup of coffee down here. (Who's taken my coffee?)
8 You should have been with us last night! (Something exciting happened last night.)
9 I liked most parts of your proposal. (There were some parts I didn't like.)

See **2** for possible replies.

2 As in the Student's Book.

ANSWERS
a	2	f	3
b	7	g	4
c	1	h	6
d	9	i	5
e	8		

3 [5.2] As in the Student's Book.

ANSWERS
The man is very direct and the woman is very indirect.
1 Introduction to the team
2 Meeting with Laura Berne
3 Lunch at a nearby restaurant
4 Review of the sales figures
5 Meeting with Julio Ramon
6 Meeting with Knut Fliedner

4 Play the recording again if necessary to enable students to identify the things the woman said that indicated she wasn't happy with the schedule. Make brief notes of them on the board so students can confirm their answers when they listen to the next recording.

5 [5.3] As in the Student's Book.

6 [5.2] When you play the recording again, ask students to stop you when they hear the woman say something that indicates she is unhappy. Find out who they think was at fault here – the woman or the man.

Note: Some cultures tend to be more direct than others, and students probably need to be able to adapt to the culture of their foreign contacts. For example, an instruction like 'Do it!' might be appropriate in Germany or Sweden, while in Britain, people would probably expect it to be framed as a request. Similarly, it may not be polite to say 'no' to a request in Japan, and people might say something like 'It's very difficult' instead.

7 Use these questions to encourage general discussion on levels of directness.

Task

1 As in the Student's Book. This is a challenging task so give students some time to think about what they can say before you ask them to start the call. In large classes, you can divide the class in half (one group of As and one group of Bs), and let them swap ideas on what to say first.

2 As in the Student's Book.

Resolving conflict

37

Quick check

Students can work through this individually or in pairs. Here is more information on the answers to **3**.

a *How are you doing?* is most commonly used as a greeting like *How are you?* in the US. British people tend to use the phrase to enquire about someone's progress on a task.

b In American English *turnover* refers to the rate at which staff join and leave a company. It can have this meaning in British English, where that rate is also called *staff turnover* or *employee turnover*. But most commonly *turnover* refers to the total income a company makes from sales in a given period (usually a year). Americans use the term *revenues* for this.

c In American English *mad* usually means *angry*. In British English, it usually means *crazy*.

d A *check* (US) or a *cheque* (UK) is the piece of paper printed by a bank that you sign and use to pay for things. In the US, the term is also used for a *bill* – a written demand for payment. So an American saying this is probably asking for a bill, e.g. in a restaurant. A British person saying this is probably asking for payment.

CAREER DILEMMAS

1 Discuss these questions with the whole class.

Quick check

ANSWERS
a 4
b 2
c 5
d 6
e 1
f 3

2 [5.4] Play the recording a couple of times if necessary and check students understand the dilemma fully before asking what they would do. If they are having difficulty, guide them with these questions:

a What new venture is her company starting? (A 'virtual' university – probably a school on the Internet.)

b What will it do? (Provide employees with distance learning course via computers.)
c What has her company asked her to do? (Lead the new venture.)
d What's the problem? (She's never done anything like it before and she loves her current job.)

Encourage students to use the phrases given to say what they would do.

3 As in the Student's Book. There are a lot of idiomatic phrases that students might find difficult in this text, so check their answers to b and c thoroughly.

ANSWERS
a Students' own answers.
b Two reasons:
He realized he was mortal and it was an opportunity to create something lasting.
He realized that he might not be tolerated indefinitely in his current job.
c Because he feels he is making a positive difference to people's lives.

4 Students' own answers. Encourage students to hypothesize here and don't insist on full conditional forms. One clause (rather than two) often sounds more natural, e.g.:

He might have stayed in his old job till he retired.
He could have taken the new job and found he didn't like it.

5 This exercise contrasts second and third conditional forms.

ANSWERS
hadn't accepted – past perfect
have regretted – present perfect
offered – simple past
accept – present

The first sentence describes an imaginary situation in the past – something that didn't happen.
The second sentence describes an imaginary situation in the future – something that's unlikely to happen.

6 [5.5] As in the Student's Book.

Resolving conflict

> **EXTRA ACTIVITY**
> 1 *This is a good time to check students know some common expressions used for giving advice, because they will have the opportunity to practise them in the task.*
>
> *Write these phrases on the board:*
> a Have you thought about …?
> b If I were you, I'd …
> c I think you should …
> d You'd better …
> e Why don't you …?
> f Your best bet is …
>
> *Ask the class:*
> 1 Which expressions are most forceful? (c and d)
> 2 Which are least forceful? (a and e)
> 3 What does 'd stand for in the expressions 'If I were you I'd…' and 'You'd better…'? (*would* and *had*)
> 4 Which phrase is followed by a gerund (an *-ing* form)? (a)
> 5 Which phrase is followed by a full infinitive form (to do)? (f NOT d)
> 2 For more dilemmas for students to consider, see **Activity 1** on page 61.

Task

1 and **2** As in the Student's Book.

NEGOTIATING

This section takes a broad interpretation of 'negotiating', providing practice in discussions where conflict needs to be resolved between people from the same organization as well as different organizations. It is suitable for students whose jobs may involve them in formal negotiations with external contacts and also for students who simply need to work alongside foreign colleagues within their organization.

> **EXTRA ACTIVITY**
> *Turn to Activity 2 on page 62 of this book to raise awareness of negotiating skills and practise some useful collocations to do with negotiating.*

1 Discuss the definitions with the whole class, asking them to give reasons and examples. Students' own answers.

2 5.6 As in the Student's Book.

> **ANSWERS**
> a 2,000 in the first year.
> b A sliding scale (a chart that makes one quantity dependent on another, so they increase and decrease together.)
> c The length of the contract.
> d Bad – it's too long.
> e They can keep looking for another distributor. They can't afford to take too long though.

3 5.6 This exercise concerns words followed by infinitive verb forms (*to do*) and gerunds (*-ing*). Students should pencil in their answers before listening to the recording again to confirm them.

> **ANSWERS**
> a to ask   e thinking
> b to increase   f looking
> c to work out   g to take
> d making

Point out that certain verbs like *intend* are followed by full infinitive forms (*to do*). Other verbs like *avoid* are followed by gerunds (*-ing*). Explain that there are no rules and they need to learn which verbs are followed by gerunds or infinitives one by one. Reassure them that they probably already know many of these verbs, particularly common ones like *want to do*, *finish doing*, etc. Also there will be more practice later in this section.

4 5.7 Before playing the recording, make sure students understand they are going to listen to the actual negotiation. You may wish to play the negotiation again.

> **ANSWERS**
> a Control over the pricing of the bicycles in American stores and a three-year exclusive contract.
> b The distributor said they thought they could sell ten thousand a year, a lot more than expected, so he is more willing to compromise.

5 Students should complete the e-mail individually, then check answers as a whole class activity.

> **ANSWERS**
> 1 signing   6 to go
> 2 to sell   7 doing
> 3 to do   8 looking
> 4 damaging   9 setting up
> 5 to carve

Resolving conflict

Whether it's wise for the bicycle manufacturer to reject the distributor's offer is debatable. The high sales predictions are very attractive but low prices could damage its reputation in its home market.

6 As in the Student's Book.

> **ANSWERS**
> a 3, 5, 9
> b 1, 6, 8
> c 2, 4, 7

Task

1 Read through all three scenarios with the class first and find out whether students have encountered any similar situations in their work. There are three scenarios, so students are likely to be able to find one that suits the context they are working in. Make sure the teams know who they are representing in each scenario.

a One team will represent the interests of the employees and the other the senior management.
b One team will represent the pharmaceutical company and the other the marketing agency.
c One team will represent the marketing division of the bank and the other the customer support staff.

In large classes different groups can act out different scenarios, and of course, students can act out more than one scenario.

> *EXTRA ACTIVITY*
> *If students would like further negotiating practice, here are two more scenarios that can be exploited in the same way as the ones in the task.*
> *1 The employees of an insurance company would like unlimited access to the Internet at work to enable them to research industry trends. Their management fear it will result in time wasting and enable viruses to get onto the system. The management currently monitors all e-mails sent and received by employees, who complain they have no privacy.*
> *2 The purchasing department thinks the company should only buy products and services from suppliers that they have approved. They say they can negotiate the best prices. But some departments want to select their suppliers themselves. They say they know what they need better than the purchasing department, so they know the best suppliers.*

2 and **3** As in the Student's Book.

GOING GLOBAL

In this section, students will read about decision-making processes in an American multinational and then take part in a meeting to decide on a globalization problem. Finally they will have the opportunity to compare the outcome of their simulated meeting with the outcome of a real meeting that tackled similar issues in similar circumstances.

1 Students do this individually then compare their opinions with the class.

2 The article can be read with the whole class, individually, or in pairs. After reading, return to the statements in **1** to check comprehension of AES's position.

> **ANSWERS**
> AES believes work should be fun, that managers should advise but not make decisions, and that specialists are a liability.

3 Students can discuss these questions in pairs or small groups, then collect answers from the whole class. Students working for multinationals with foreign parent companies may be able to contribute first-hand experiences of differing value systems.

4 As in the Student's Book.

> **ANSWERS**
> 1 *Boring* describes a quality something has.
> 2 *Bored* describes a reaction to something else.

Point out that these adjectives are both formed from the verb *to bore*. Many English verbs have two adjective forms like this, e.g. *surprised, surprising*. Ask students to think of some more and write them on the board.

5 If necessary, remind students that adjectives ending in *-ed* usually describe how people feel. Adjectives ending in *-ing* usually describe the people or things that caused the feelings.

Resolving conflict

ANSWERS

1	interesting	6	frustrating
2	amazed	7	surprised
3	boring	8	astonished
4	fulfilling	9	worrying
5	threatened	10	interested

EXTRA DISCUSSION QUESTION
Have you ever had similar feelings to this manager?

Task

1 As in the Student's Book. Check that students understand the meaning of:

layoffs: redundancies; cases where people lose their jobs because there is no longer work available
a voluntary redundancy scheme: a plan or system where workers choose to give up their jobs or agree to stop working for a company, often because there are financial incentives to do so
to overrule: to decide that another person's decisions or actions are not valid

Note: Although common in British English, *make redundant* is not used in American English. Americans say *lay off* instead. *Lay off* is used in British English too, but strictly speaking the two expressions have a slight difference in meaning. *Laying off* is a temporary action and workers may be re-employed later while *making redundant* is permanent. However in practice, *lay off* has become a euphemism for *make redundant*.

2 At the end of the task, students are directed to a reading text about a similar meeting in File 15 on page 62. There are no comprehension questions for the reading text in the Student's Book. Students' understanding is checked by asking them to compare the outcomes of this meeting with their own outcomes. However, if you wish to ask more detailed questions or guide their understanding, use these questions:

- What joint venture did AES enter in 1992? (They teamed up with a Belgian utility company to buy two power plants in Ireland.)
- Is the venture successful? (Financially yes, but culturally it has been more difficult.)
- What do Irish managers find frustrating about the new culture and why? (They don't like standing by and watching front-line workers make decisions. Presumably it's because they feel their long and hard gained experience is not being put to good use.)
- What disagreement did they have about replacing a steel pipe? (The operators wanted to replace it with a cheaper plastic one. The managers didn't.)
- Was the problem resolved successfully? (Yes. The operators won, used a plastic pipe and one year on, the pipe is still fine.)
- What disagreement did they have about laying workers off? (A manager from the US parent company wanted to announce one big lay off. The local managers wanted a voluntary redundancy program instead.)
- Was the problem resolved successfully? (No. The local management won, but not enough workers volunteered. It took five years to shrink the work force.)
- Who is Dennis Bakke and what did he say about it? (The CEO of AES and he said, 'The managers just didn't trust the workers enough to turn over power'.)

EXTRA ACTIVITY
Turn to Activity 3 on page 63 of this book for an activity that helps to raise cross-cultural awareness and gives socializing practice.

WORKING ACROSS CULTURES

As teachers and trainers, we walk a dangerous tight rope when we tackle cultural issues in the classroom. If we focus on similarities between cultures, we may fail to warn students of potential areas of misunderstanding. If we focus on differences, we may encourage stereotyping. But to achieve an understanding of other cultures, learners probably need to become aware of their own and this activity can provide some useful insights, as well as recycling language from earlier in this unit and book.

1 As in the Student's Book.

2 Draw attention to the words *individualist* and *group-minded* in questions a and b, as students will probably find these words useful in the discussions that follow.

Resolving conflict

ANSWERS
a The results vary from question to question but the USA, Russia, and Spain seem to have the most individualist cultures.
b France and Thailand seem to be the most 'group-minded' countries.
c, d, and e Students' own answers.

Here are some more of Trompenaars' results for other countries:

	Italy	Finland	Egypt	Greece	Austria	China
Question 1	52%	65%	41%	49%	56%	64%

	Italy	Portugal	Belgium	Finland	Argentina	Nigeria
Question 2	20%	25%	27%	34%	37%	13%
Question 3	38%	49%	40%	26%	41%	55%

It appears that only the data for Question 3 was collected post reunification of Germany, while that for Questions 1 and 2 is from earlier.

3 Discuss these questions with the whole class.

4 Students read the e-mail. They can discuss the answer to the question with a partner, before you collect their answers.

ANSWERS
The Vice President wants them to:
– attend a one day meeting to decide how the pay of sales forces can be standardized on a global basis.
– be prepared to explain how pay is currently calculated in their territory.

Because:
They want to improve efficiency. (Presumably the differing pay systems that currently exist are not efficient.)

5 Ask stude
customer sa
ratings, admi
(which is imp
etc.

6 Depending
representative
far as possible,
countries they

7 There is no
compromise se
conclude (as m
decisions about
rewards need to
a local basis.

Resolving conflict

Unit 1

Activity 1 — False facts game

1 You're going to get to know some of your fellow students better. Before you begin, think of two things you do or have done that might be interesting to other students in the class. For example, are you involved in local politics, do you come from an unusually large family, are you writing a book? Or have you won a golf tournament, appeared on television, or been in prison? As well as thinking of two interesting facts that are true, also invent one unusual fact about yourself that isn't true. Write them here:

True fact 1 _____

_____

True fact 2 _____

_____

False fact _____

_____

2 Work in small groups with some other students and get better acquainted. Choose one or two of the topics below to talk about. Everyone should try to introduce their two true facts and one false fact into the conversation. Listen carefully to others in the group – try to spot their false facts.

- Your jobs and current projects
- Your career histories
- Families, schools, and education
- Places you have lived or visited
- Free time, interests, and sports

3 What interesting things did you learn about your fellow students? Did you discover anything you have in common? Did you spot the false information? Write it down for each person then check if you were right.

Student's name	False fact	Anything in common?

Photocopiable © Oxford University Press

Unit 1

Activity 2

Collocations with *take*

1 Look at the texts about Toyota, FedEx, and 3M on page 7 of the Student's Book again and identify some common expressions with the verb *take*.

2 Think of some more expressions with the verb *take*, e.g. *take a chance*.

3 We use the verb *take* in many expressions. Here are some important meanings:

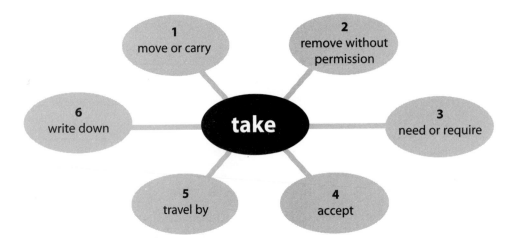

Match the verbs in *italics* in the sentences below to a meaning above.
e.g. *Let's **take** the train.* (*take* means *travel by*)
a It only *takes* five days. ....
b *Take* some cash with you. ....
c I'll *take* the minutes of the meeting. ....
d Do you *take* American Express? ....
e Who's *taken* my pen? ....

Now check your answers at the bottom of this page.

Answers

1 Toyota: *take delivery*, Fedex: *to take care of a customer*, 3M: *to take initiative, take risks*

2 There are lots of possible expressions with *take*. Here are some common ones: *to take a look at something / a moment / advantage of something / pride in something / an opportunity / time*

In many languages *take* is used in expressions like *to take some coffee*, where in English we would say *to have some coffee*. *Take* sounds strange in English in this expression. For more information on expressions like this, see page 73 in the Student's Book.

3 a 3, b 1, c 6, d 4, e 2

Unit 1 — Activity 3: Missions

1 These objectives come from the mission statements of seven different organizations. With a partner, work out what sort of organization each one might be.

a To minimize the loss of life and property from fires, medical emergencies, and environmental disasters through prevention, education, fire suppression, medical services, rescue skills, and other emergency and non-emergency activities.

b To supply reliable, low-cost gas and electricity services to our customers while making optimal use of our resources to ensure profitable growth for our shareholders.

c To maintain public trust and continually employ cutting-edge technology to improve and enhance our products, services, and the security of our games and systems.

d To provide efficient, comprehensive health care services, educate and train health professionals, and to foster research in order to advance professional knowledge.

e To increase public awareness of the importance and value of river ecosystems and to strengthen community-based efforts to protect them.

f To provide policies that meet our clients' financial needs in order to give them peace of mind and freedom from insecurity.

g To find, evaluate, select, organize, describe, and create quality information resources.

to facilitate to make something possible or easier
foster help and encourage something to develop
optimal the best

2 Select words from the boxes below to formulate some objectives for different sections of your organization(s). You can change words and include other phrases where appropriate, such as those used in the texts in **1**. Try to include some adverbs as well.

e.g. *The objective of the IT group is to **maintain reliable** computer systems **efficiently** in order to **facilitate** access to **accurate information**.*

Their objective/goal/ mission is to …	maximize	maximum	systems
	foster	reliable	services
	initiate	accurate	research
	ensure	creative	technology
	facilitate	innovative	improvements
	maintain	professional	products
in order to …	create	profitable	information
	provide	efficient	growth
	develop	cost effective	resources

3 What are your personal goals in life? Write an objective or mission statement for your life. In one sentence, identify who you are, what you do, and what your objectives are. When you have finished, compare your statement with some other students. Whose is the most interesting?

Photocopiable © Oxford University Press

Unit 1 Activity 4 — Teamwork

1 How important is teamwork in your job? What teams are you a member of? Do they work well? What factors are important in building an effective team?

2 Have you ever heard of General Electric? What do you know about the company? Read how General Electric builds good team relationships. Do you do anything similar in your company?

Getting to know you – fast

In a recent survey, *The Financial Times* named General Electric the most respected company in the world. Operating in more than 100 countries, GE manages to make money in widely diverse industries such as broadcasting, aircraft engines, kitchen and laundry equipment, and financial services.

Helping to facilitate that success is Bill Hunt, a senior human resources executive at GE Power Systems. He runs accelerated relationship-building activities with new managers and employees that are practised in GE divisions around the world. Says Bill, 'They're super-intensive getting-to-know-you meetings that reduce by three to six months the time it normally takes to build an effective team.'

'First, without the manager present, I meet with team members to help them generate questions: What do we know about the new manager? The answer can be anything from "She relies on email" to "He seems to change his mind a lot." What are some things that we'd like to know? People ask all sorts of things like, "What pushes your hot buttons?" or "Are you a Republican?" This stage can generate as many as 100 questions.'

The next step is a quick meeting between Bill and the new manager to review the issues raised. Then the manager makes an off-the-cuff presentation in front of the team. 'It's remarkable how much is handled on the spot,' says Bill. 'Managers often cover 98 out of 100 items. Sometimes they really bare their souls. The meeting becomes a great bonding experience.'

These meetings compress months of getting-to-know-you into a few highly charged hours. 'It's the best way to iron out rumours and to create a climate of openness,' says Bill.

---

accelerated speeded up, made faster
to **bare their souls** to reveal their true nature and deep feelings
bonding joining with feelings of friendship
to **compress** to make something shorter and briefer
diverse very different from each other
highly charged very emotional

to **iron out** to solve something that's causing difficulty
off-the-cuff spontaneous, without previous preparation
to **push a hot button** to cause anger
a **rumour** news that many people are talking about that's possibly not true
a **survey** a study of something

---

3 Why do you think this activity is so successful at GE? Do you think it could be effective in your organization? Why/Why not?

Unit 1

Activity 4 (cont.) — Teamwork

4 Here are the answers to some questions about the article. Write down the questions?
e.g. GE Power Systems.
What section of General Electric does Bill Hunt work for?

a He's a senior human resources executive.
_____

b It stands for General Electric.
_____

c They're for building good working relationships between new managers and their teams.
_____

d All sorts.
_____

e Just a few hours.
_____

f They cover lots of ground, they're highly charged, and great bonding experiences.
_____

Now match these questions to the right answers above.

1 What sorts of questions do people ask?
2 How long do the meetings last?
3 What does GE stand for?
4 What's Bill's job?
5 What are the meetings like?
6 What are the meetings for?

5 Imagine you're going to be working with a new manager. Conduct a similar getting-to-know-you activity. Begin by choosing a facilitator like Bill Hunt. Then brainstorm these questions:

a What would you like to know about the new manager and their management style?
b What questions do you want to ask them? The facilitator should make a note of your questions.

6 Now work individually. Imagine you're going to become the manager of a new team. Prepare a two-minute presentation covering some of the questions you brainstormed. You can make notes, but don't write full sentences. Just write key words.

7 Take it in turns to deliver your presentations – either to the whole class or to small groups.

Unit 1

Activity 5 — Presentation notes

Use this sheet to make notes on the presentation you will hear.

Interesting points I didn't know:

Questions I want to ask:

	needs work	good	really good	excellent
Are the ideas well organized?				
Is the speaker clear?				
Is the timing and pacing good?				
Are they doing a professional job?				
Does the audience want to listen?				
Do they handle questions well?				

Unit 2

Activity 1

Brainstorming

1 In what ways do you have to be creative in your job? What do you do when you're stuck for ideas? Read these extracts from articles about what people do at IBM and IDEO. Which ideas might work for you? Are there any you would (or wouldn't) like to try?

IBM must be one of the most creative companies there is, but even so, their people sometimes get stuck for ideas. So IBM researchers have produced a handbook filled with tips for their colleagues to make the creative process easier. Consider, for example, tip number 48: *'Brainstorm with someone 10 years older and someone 10 years younger.'*

At IBM, coming up with creative ideas seems to be a fairly peaceful activity. The next time you're stuck for an idea, you might want to try tip number 30 from the handbook: *'Leave the office. Sit with just a pencil and a pad of paper. See what happens.'* Or maybe tip number 32 is better: *'Go for a bike ride'*.

Brainstorming is popular at IDEO, arguably the most influential design company in the world. In a network of offices stretching from San Francisco to London to Tokyo, 250 IDEO employees create around 90 new products a year, ranging from window blinds and toothpaste containers to cutting-edge laptop computers, and virtual reality headgear.

IDEO has special brainstorming rooms where its guiding principles appear on the walls. *Stay focused on the topic ... Encourage wild ideas ... Defer judgement ... Build on the ideas of others ... One conversation at a time.*

Employees can draw pictures on whiteboard-covered walls and tables and the meetings generate a frenzy of activity. The company quickly prototypes the most promising ideas so it can learn from the ones that don't work. As the CEO, David Kelly puts it, *'We fail faster in order to succeed sooner.'*

cutting-edge the most advanced position
to **defer** to leave something until a later time
a **frenzy** a state of great excitement
headgear clothing or equipment worn on the head
influential having influence
promising showing signs of being successful
to be **stuck** unable to solve a problem because it's difficult

2 Work in small groups. Look through these topics and select some that interest you.

- The best things to do when you're stuck for ideas
- Ways to make your office or work space more fun
- Things that make meetings more productive
- The most useful ways to spend $15
- The most useful ways to spend 15 minutes
- Different ways for governments to tax people
- Different ways in which you can earn more income
- Activities that help you learn English more quickly

3 Decide how to record your ideas, then hold short brainstorming sessions on the topics. When you've finished, tell the rest of the class about them. Which group had:

a the most ideas?   **b** the best ideas?   **c** the most original ideas?

Photocopiable © Oxford University Press

Unit 2 Activity 2 — Evaluating ideas

Student A

You work for Distrilux. Read what's been happening in this company and tell your partner about it in your own words. Find out if their organization does anything similar to this already. Ask if it would work if they implemented the same idea.

> Distrilux, the sea distribution subsidiary of Electrolux, has become the first company within the group to conduct all its business over the Internet. 'If Distrilux's suppliers are not online, they cannot do business with us any more,' said Anders Edholm, head of Internet developments at Electrolux.

Student B

Read what's been happening on the American Family Association web page and tell your partner about it in your own words. Find out if their organization does anything similar to this already. Ask if it would work if they implemented the same idea.

> From the American Family Association web page:
> 'We apologize, but due to the overwhelming amount of requests we are getting per day, we are no longer able to receive correspondence by e-mail. Please contact us via snail mail or phone …'

overwhelming very great
snail mail letters that are written and sent on paper, not from one computer to another

Unit 2

Activity 3

Procedures

1 What sort of meetings do (or will) you attend at work that are held in English? Are they for:

making decisions?
passing on information?
brainstorming ideas?
planning events?
solving problems?
something else (what?)

2 Work with a partner. Take it in turns to interview one another about the meetings. Find out about:

the purpose	
when they're held	
how long they last	
who attends	
pre-meeting preparations	
the chair (How is the chair chosen? Do you have one?, etc.)	
the agenda (Who prepares it? Do you follow it?, etc.)	
snacks or refreshments	
the dress code	

3 What are (will be) the main problems you face?

Photocopiable © Oxford University Press

Unit 3

Activity 1 — Reporting problems

---

1 I've been up all night working on this report …

2 My car's run out of petrol …

3 We've run out of transformers …

4 One of our customers has gone bankrupt …

5 Management has brought the deadline forward …

6 The euro's fallen against the dollar …

… so I'm very tired.

… so I can't get to work.

… so we can't produce the order.

… so they can't pay their bill.

… so we haven't got much time.

… so American goods will cost more.

---

a I should have gone home hours ago.

b I should have filled it up last night, but I forgot.

c We should have ordered more.

d We shouldn't have given them credit.

e We should have allocated more people to the job.

f We should have bought ahead on the currency market.

---

52 Photocopiable © Oxford University Press

Unit 3 Activity 2 — Polite requests and offers

1 Your customer is carrying a heavy suitcase. Offer to help.

2 Ask a colleague if they'd like to read a 600-page report you've just written called 'How to improve productivity'.

3 You want your colleague to help you put 5,000 letters in envelopes for a direct mailshot.

4 You're travelling without your laptop computer. Ask if you can use your colleague's computer to check your e-mail.

5 Invite a friend to have lunch with you in a local restaurant.

6 Your friend's car won't start. Offer to give it a push.

7 You are having an 'open day' at work. Find out whether your customer wants to come.

8 Ask a friend if you can use their mobile phone. (You want to call your cousin in Australia.)

9 Your colleague's car is being serviced tomorrow. Offer to give them a lift/ride to work.

10 Ask another student if you can borrow $10.

11 Ask another student to lend you $1,000.

12 You've lost your Student's Book. Ask another student if you can borrow theirs.

Photocopiable © Oxford University Press   53

Unit 3 Activity 3 — Correspondence

1 What correspondence do you send or receive in English? Who do you communicate with and what about?

2 Do you have an English grammar and spell checker on your computer and do you use it? Here are some rules for writing. What rules do they break? Work with a partner and correct them. Which rules do you think are most important?

WRITING RULES

1 Verbs has to agree with their subjects.
2 No sentences without verbs.
3 Don't include commas, that are, not necessary.
4 Use the apostrophe in it's proper place and don't use it when its not needed.
5 Don't repeat yourself and don't say the same thing twice.
6 Allways check your speling.
7 Check carefully to see if you any words out.

3 Below are some formal phrases we might use in correspondence to someone we don't know very well. Match each one to a more informal alternative in 1–8.

a I'm writing to enquire whether …
b With reference to …
c I would be grateful if you could …
d If you wish, we would be happy to …
e I apologize for …
f Please find attached …
g If I can be of any further assistance, please do not hesitate to ask.
h I look forward to seeing you on the 15th.

1 Do you want me to …?
2 See you soon.
3 Just a quick note to ask if …
4 About …
5 Say if you need any more help.
6 Sorry about …
7 Can you …?
8 I'm attaching …

4 Work with a partner. Cover up the formal phrases and look at the informal ones. Can you recall the more formal alternatives?

5 Try using some of the phrases. Think of a short piece of correspondence that you need to send in your job and write a draft. Hand it to another student and see if they can spot any mistakes.

Unit 3

Activity 4 — Keep talking

Student A

1 Sometimes we need to tell people what we're doing when we're talking on the phone, so they understand if there's a delay. Here are some phrases for explaining a silence:

> I'm just getting the right papers/writing that down/looking it up/calling it up on my screen.
>
> Someone's at the door/on the other line.
>
> Please bear with me while I find out.

Can you think of any more reasons?

2 Your colleague will call you to ask some questions. The answers to the questions are all in your Student's Book somewhere. You will need to keep your partner talking while you look for them. Try to answer their questions as fast as you can and try to keep talking. Explain any short silences.

3 Call your colleague and ask for the following information. Make a note of their answers. You can give them the clues in brackets if they need help.

   a Ask your partner to tell you what the Japanese word 'kaizen' means in English. (See page 7)
   b You want to find out how much time off work employees at AFLAC can have, if they need to care for a sick husband, wife, child, or parent. (See page 28)
   c You know lasers were invented in 1960 and they are now employed in all sorts of applications such as metal cutters and CD players but you want to know the name of the person who invented them. (See page 19)
   d You need to know the meaning of the English phrase 'lead time'. (See page 77)
   e Animation Magic Inc. hired Russian artists to work as computer animators. You want to know how much they paid them. (See page 21)
   f Ask your partner when 'minimill' technology was invented. (See page 40)

If your partner is very slow, hurry them along:

> I'm afraid I'm in a hurry.
> I'm afraid I don't have much time.
> I'm afraid I have a meeting in a minute.

If your partner is silent for too long say:

> Hello? Hello?
> Are you still there?
> I'm afraid I must go now. I'll call again later.

4 Check your partner's answers below, and ask them whether you got all the answers to their questions right.

Answers
   a continuous improvement   d the time between placing an order and receiving a product
   b 12 weeks   e $2,100 a year
   c Theodore Maiman   f in the mid-1960s

Photocopiable © Oxford University Press

Unit 3 Activity 4 — Keep talking

Student B

1 Sometimes we need to tell people what we're doing when we're talking on the phone, so they understand if there's a delay. Here are some phrases for explaining a silence:

> *I'm just getting the right papers/writing that down/looking it up/calling it up on my screen.*
>
> *Someone's at the door/on the other line.*
>
> *Please bear with me while I find out.*

Can you think of any more reasons?

2 Call your colleague, ask for the following information, and make a note of their answers. You can give them the clues in brackets if they need help.

- a You need to know how many aircraft the transportation company FedEx has. (See page 6)
- b You know Johannes Gutenburg invented the printing press, but you've forgotten when. (See page 19)
- c You need to know the meaning of the English word 'diligent'. (See page 76)
- d You want to know the name of the Harvard professor who developed the theory of disruptive technologies. (See page 41)
- e Some companies have been providing places for their employees to take a nap (short sleep). You want to find out which companies have been experimenting with this. (See page 21)
- f Ask your partner what country the movie *Gorillas in the Mist* was filmed in? (See page 26)

If your partner is very slow, hurry them along:

> *I'm afraid I'm in a hurry.*
> *I'm afraid I don't have much time.*
> *I'm afraid I have a meeting in a minute.*

If your partner is silent for too long say:

> *Hello? Hello?*
> *Are you still there?*
> *I'm afraid I must go now. I'll call again later.*

3 Now it's your turn. (Oh dear!) Your colleague will call you to ask some questions. The answers to the questions are all in your Student's Book somewhere. You will need to keep your partner talking while you look for them. Try to answer their questions as fast as you can and try to keep talking. Explain any short silences.

4 Check your partner's answers below, and ask them whether you got all the answers to their questions right.

Answers

- a 650
- b 1450
- c showing care and effort in your work
- d Professor Clayton Christensen
- e Gould Evans Goodman Associates and Yarde Metals
- f Rwanda

Unit 4

Activity 1 — Describing trends

Student A

1 Match theses sentences to the appropriate graph.

  a Sales rose dramatically.
  b There was a sharp drop in exports.
  c Inflation fell slightly.

2 Fill in the missing prepositions.

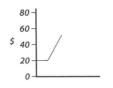

Prices rose .... $50.   *Prices rose .... $50.*

3 Tell your partner how these share prices changed between January and June. Then, your partner will tell you how they changed from July to December. Listen and complete the graph.

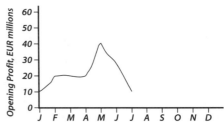

Student B

1 Match theses sentences to the appropriate graph.

  a Sales rose dramatically.
  b There was a sharp drop in exports.
  c Inflation fell slightly.

2 Fill in the missing prepositions.

Prices rose .... $50.   *Prices rose .... $50.*

3 Your partner will describe how these share prices changed between January and June. Listen and complete the graph. Then tell your partner how they changed from July to December.

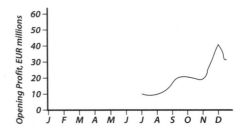

Photocopiable © Oxford University Press

Unit 4

Activity 2 — Arranging schedules

Student A

1 You are news producers at a television station and you're scheduling your outside camera crews for the day. Here are today's events. Which ones do you think sound interesting? Which ones do you think you should cover?

- A visit to your town by the president.
- An environmental group protest outside a biotech company.
- An interview with a popular foreign actress.
- The opening of the new Symphony Hall.
- A police investigation of a bank robbery.
- 200 workers being laid off at a chocolate factory.
- The mayor's speech.
- An interview with a firefighter who rescued a cat from a tree.

2 Luckily you have three camera crews so you can cover all the stories. Exchange your information with your partner and work out a schedule together. Pencil in the times.

President's visit: Today's top story – shoot the whole thing.
Environmental protest: It'll take 2 hours to get shots of the protesters and interviews.
Actress: You have an appointment with her for 3 p.m.
New Symphony Hall: Shoot the ribbon being cut – one hour's work.
Bank robbery: You can do this any time.
Chocolate factory: 5 p.m. is best – to get shots of workers leaving.
Mayor: It depends how long the speech lasts – 1 or 2 hours' work.
Firefighter: It'll only take an hour to interview him.

	Crew 1	Crew 2	Crew 3
11 a.m.–12 a.m.			
12 a.m.–1 p.m.			
1 p.m.–2 p.m.			
2 p.m.–3 p.m.			
3 p.m.–4 p.m.			
4 p.m.–5 p.m.			
5 p.m.–6 p.m.			

3 It's 11 a.m. and you've just heard that a fire's started at a local hospital. You must send one of your camera crews there all day. You can drop the stories about the mayor and the new Symphony Hall, but you should schedule all the others. Work with your partner again and rearrange the schedule. (It is possible!)

Photocopiable © Oxford University Press

Unit 4

Activity 2 — Arranging schedules

Student B

1 You are news producers at a television station and you're scheduling your outside camera crews for the day. Here are today's events. Which ones do you think sound interesting? Which ones do you think you should cover?

- A visit to your town by the president.
- An environmental group protest outside a biotech company.
- An interview with a popular foreign actress.
- The opening of the new Symphony Hall.
- A police investigation of a bank robbery.
- 200 workers being laid off at a chocolate factory.
- The mayor's speech.
- An interview with a firefighter who rescued a cat from a tree.

2 Luckily you have three camera crews so you can cover all the stories. Exchange your information with your partner and draw up a schedule together. Pencil in the times.

President's visit: She's arriving at 1 p.m. and staying all day.
Environmental protest: Going on all day so shoot it any time.
Actress: It'll only take an hour to interview her.
New Symphony Hall: The opening ceremony is at 12 p.m.
Bank robbery: You want shots of the bank and interviews – 4 hours' work.
Chocolate factory: This will probably take an hour to shoot.
Mayor: His speech is scheduled to start at 11 a.m.
Firefighter: He's free for interviews any time (not sure about the cat).

	Crew 1	Crew 2	Crew 3
11 a.m.–12 a.m.			
12 a.m.–1 p.m.			
1 p.m.–2 p.m.			
2 p.m.–3 p.m.			
3 p.m.–4 p.m.			
4 p.m.–5 p.m.			
5 p.m.–6 p.m.			

3 It's 11 a.m. and you've just heard that a fire's started at a local hospital. You must send one of your camera crews there all day. You can drop the stories about the mayor and the new Symphony Hall, but you should schedule all the others. Work with your partner again and rearrange the schedule. (It is possible!)

Photocopiable © Oxford University Press

Unit 4 Activity 3 — Collocations dominoes

GAME 1

a company	stay on
staff	meet
new technology	implement
insurance	surrender
schedule	go
a deadline	be under
changes	negotiate
control	complete

bankrupt	reach
pressure	launch
a deal	sign
a project	upgrade
a target	train
a new product	invest in
a contract	take out
a product	found

Unit 5

Activity 1 — Ethical dilemmas

Work in small groups. Read the dilemmas below and discuss the questions that follow.

Dilemma 1
A friend you play tennis with works for a pharmaceutical company. They happen to mention in passing that a new drug the company has developed is about to be approved for distribution by the government. You are sure the company's stocks are going to rise dramatically when the news breaks.

a Would you buy some of the company's stocks?
b Should your friend have mentioned this?
c Should you have said anything about it when they did?

Dilemma 2
Your company's new Head of Purchasing is very hard working, a great negotiator, and also very popular with her staff. However, you recently witnessed a conversation in which one of her team showed her a bottle of champagne that they had been given by a supplier. She told the employee it probably wasn't worth much so it was OK to keep it, although your company policy states employees should not accept gifts.

a Was the Head of Purchasing's response correct? If not, would you do anything about it? If so, what?
b What would you have done if you'd been the purchasing manager and a member of your team had shown you the champagne?
c What would you do if you received a similar gift from a customer?

Dilemma 3
You were sitting near some of your competitors in a restaurant recently and you couldn't help overhearing some of their conversation. They were discussing a problem they were having with a product. Later, you visit a customer who tells you that they are thinking of buying your competitors' product instead of yours.

a Would you tell your customer about the problem you heard discussed? Why/Why not?
b When you were in the restaurant, should you have moved to another table to avoid overhearing, or did it not matter?
c Have you ever encountered a similar situation to this? If so, what happened?

Dilemma 4
You are a responsible for the buildings of your company's largest factory and you regularly employ building contractors to do maintenance and building work. You've just bought a new house and it needs some work. You asked one of your company's regular contractors to give you a price estimate for the work on your house. The estimate has arrived and it is much lower than the market rate.

a Should you have asked one of the company's builders for a price estimate for work on your private house?
b Would you accept the estimate and employ the builder? Why/Why not?
c If the builder told you the estimate was low because it included the standard discount your company gets, would you employ him?

Photocopiable © Oxford University Press

Unit 5 Activity 2 — Negotiating skills

1 What do you need to do to be successful in a negotiation? Match the starts and ends of these quotations.

a	To be prepared …	1	everyone believes that he has got the biggest piece. *(Ludwig Erhard)*
b	There are no big problems.	2	has the loudest voice. *(Leroy Brownlow)*
c	A compromise is the art of dividing a cake in such a way that …	3	is half the victory. *(Miguel De Cevantes)*
d	The fellow who says he'll meet you halfway usually thinks …	4	you can never cancel it and put things back the way they are. *(Howard Hughes)*
e	Once you consent to some concession, …	5	so we could hear twice as much as we speak. *(Epictetus)*
f	There are times when silence …	6	Just a lot of little problems. *(Henry Ford)*
g	Nature gave us one tongue and two ears …	7	he's standing on the dividing line. *(Orlando A Batista)*

a **concession** something you agree to do or give up in order to end an argument
to **consent** to agree to something

a **compromise** an agreement that is reached when each side allows the other side part of what it wanted

2 Suggest different verbs we could use with these nouns.

   a to _____ an agreement   b to _____ a compromise   c to _____ a concession

e.g. *to come to an agreement, to make an agreement*
Read these lists of verbs. Match each list to one of the nouns above.

1 to win, to consent to, to get, to agree to
2 to look for, to find, to agree on
3 to break, to cancel, to sign, to enter into

3 Which of the two nouns in 2 above go with these verbs?

to come to, to reach, to work out, to arrive at

4 What advice do the quotations in 1 contain for negotiators and do you think it's valuable? What other advice might you give someone who had to take part in a difficult negotiation?

Answers
1 a 3, b 6, c 1, d 7, e 4, f 2, g 5
2 a 3, b 2, c 1
3 We use the verbs with *an agreement* and *a compromise*

Unit 5 — Activity 3 — International meetings

1 How do meetings start in your company? Do they start on time? What does everyone talk about while they're waiting for people to arrive?

2 Richard D Lewis, the chairman of an international institute of cross-cultural and language training, has constructed the chart below to show how meetings start around the world. Put these countries in the right place on the chart?

   a USA   b Germany   c Spain and Italy   d Japan   e UK   f France

1	Formal introduction, sit down, and begin.
2	Informal introduction, cup of coffee, wisecrack, and begin.
3	Formal introduction, cup of tea and biscuits, 10 minutes small talk (about the weather, how comfortable people are and sport), and a casual beginning.
4	Formal introduction, 15 minutes small talk (about politics and scandal), and begin.
5	Formal introduction, the seating of participants, green tea, 15–20 minutes small talk (harmonious pleasantries), a sudden signal from the senior person, and begin.
6	20–30 minutes small talk (about football and family matters) while everyone arrives. Begin when everyone is finally there.

minutes 0   5   10   15   20   25   30

a **wisecrack** a joke

3 Is your nationality mentioned in the chart? If so, do you agree with Richard Lewis? If not, what do you think he would say about your country?

4 You are going to act out the start of an international meeting. Your company took over team B's company and you're going to meet their management for the first time. It was a hostile takeover, but you would now like to form the best possible working relationship you can. You suspect there will be bad feeling on their side, however.

They sent a taxi to pick you up at your hotel early this morning. It took a while for everyone to get ready though, so you're a little late. In your culture, meetings generally start when everyone has arrived. This can take half an hour or so, which gives plenty of time for tea, biscuits, and social conversation before the meeting. One of the items on today's agenda is sales targets and budgets but you would rather not discuss that until everyone has got to know one another better socially and established a good rapport. Get together with your colleagues and discuss what you might talk about at the start of the meeting and what you can do to establish a good rapport.

Answers
1 Germany 2 USA 3 UK 4 France 5 Japan 6 Spain and Italy

Photocopiable © Oxford University Press